A Gift of Mourning Glories

A Gift of Mourning Glories

Restoring Your Life After Loss

Georgia Shaffer

SERVANT PUBLICATIONS
ANN ARBOR, MICHIGAN

Vine Books is an imprint of Servant Publications especially designed to serve evan-gelical Christians.

To protect the privacy of some of the individuals whose stories are told in this book, names and characterizations have been fictionalized, although they are based on real events. With permission, real names and events are portrayed in most of the stories.

Published by Servant Publications
P.O. Box 8617
Ann Arbor, Michigan 48107

Cover design and illustration: Hile Illustration and Design, Ann Arbor, Michigan

00 01 02 03 10 9 8 7 6 5 4 3 2

Printed in the United States of America
ISBN 1-56955-186-3

Cataloging-in-Publication Data on file at the Library of Congress.

To my son Kyle:
together we lived through our losses
and together we began anew

Contents

Acknowledgments

Although my name is on the title page, I couldn't have completed this book without those who shared their stories, others who critiqued and edited the manuscript, my mother who tirelessly provided anything and everything, and CLASS (Christian Leaders, Authors, & Speakers Services), which helped me connect with a publisher. I give my deepest thanks to each of you.

Introduction

Have you ever been lost or traveling in unfamiliar territory and needed directions?

Years ago, in an effort to save money, I stayed at my brother's home while attending a conference in Vermont. He lived in a rural area and the directions to the conference listed only major highways, so my sister-in-law told me, "I'm not certain the directions I gave you are the best, but they should get you there."

As I drove for an hour over bumpy country roads, I had the nagging feeling there *was* a better way. But when I inquired at the conference, no one could provide me with another route.

The following morning my borrowed car failed to start. I called emergency road service, and the kind man who arrived not only fixed the car but also gave me different directions to the meeting.

"I go that way all the time," he said. "Not everyone is familiar with those roads, but it's definitely a shorter and easier route."

I'm glad I met him because his expertise saved me forty minutes of traveling time that day. The experience reminded me that the most beneficial advice is obtained from someone who not only realizes *where* we are coming from but who also understands *where* we want to go.

After a recurrence of cancer, a divorce, and the loss of my job because I was too weak to work, I sensed the advice I was being given about recovery was from those who weren't familiar with the process of beginning anew. *A Gift of Mourning Glories* is the book I wanted to read during those dark, despairing years. I needed a book that was practical and inspirational. But most importantly I yearned for a book that was written by someone who had "been there" and who had successfully made the journey from devastating loss.

Has your life fallen apart, or do you know someone who has endured difficult times? Restoring our lives after loss is a skill all of us need but few of us are taught.

The outline in this book reflects what I learned as I worked toward a new life. I use analogies from my garden because God used my garden and my love of flowers to teach me many valuable lessons during these years.

My garden originally consisted of the traditional foundation plantings—generic would best describe the beds surrounding my house.

In the spring of 1990, after lengthy cancer treatments, which included a bone marrow transplant, I found myself physically debilitated and psychologically depressed. An unwanted gift of morning glory seeds led to the development of my present garden. There I found solace and wisdom.

It has only been recently that I have realized how clearly the growth of my now extensive garden reflects not only my own restoration but God's ability to transform the seemingly most hopeless of circumstances.

The simple five-step outline in *A Gift of Mourning Glories* can be applied to any troubling situation and will guide you through the journey from hurt to healing.

Give Yourself Time to Grieve

Investigate and Observe

Find the Value

Take the Risk

Share Your Gifts

Chapter One

 An Unwanted Gift

A promise is a promise, and I had promised my ten-year-old son that I'd make his favorite breakfast—blueberry pancakes.

But as I groped my way toward the kitchen doing the slipper shuffle, I had second thoughts. It was only a few months after my bone marrow transplant for a recurrence of breast cancer, and for me, making pancakes was akin to weeding an overgrown twenty-acre garden. I knew that one simple task would deplete my energy and cause me to spend the remainder of the day resting.

I thought how difficult the last few years had been for Kyle and me. I had already been through my father's death when cancer hit me. Then came a bone marrow transplant and the loss of my job and my marriage. Kyle desperately needed me to be stronger. I figured it was good for both of us to pretend things were normal even if it was only for a brief time.

I removed a quart of milk and a carton of eggs from the refrigerator. I lifted a canister of flour off the shelf and placed it beside the other ingredients, when a pack of flower seeds caught my attention.

My disposition immediately soured.

For the last several weeks that packet of morning glory seeds had lain next to the box of tissues. They were an unwanted gift from my Aunt Cecelia.

My aunt, who is like a second mother to me, loves to give. She gives gifts for all occasions and for no occasion at all.

The day she gave me the seeds I silently moaned, *Morning glory seeds? I don't have any place in my garden for a climbing plant. Why didn't she give me daisies or zinnias, anything but a climbing plant?*

However, I couldn't throw the seeds away. They were a gift for my garden.

I considered purchasing something I had always wanted—a trellis or some arch-type structure. But, with limited strength and dwindling finances, a trellis was out of the question.

Now each morning I gazed at that packet of seeds with irritation. Knowing Aunt Cecelia would ask about them, I began contriving reasons why she wouldn't see any morning glories in my garden.

"Well, Aunt Cecelia, it's like this. I had the seeds on the kitchen counter when I accidentally knocked over a pitcher of water. The seeds were drenched and had to be thrown away."

I stirred the ingredients.

Or how about, "You remember that packet of morning glory seeds you gave me? Well, I put those seeds in a very special place but now I can't find them."

The truth was, all these limp excuses made me feel uncomfortable.

I turned on the stove.

Well, if I don't find a place for these seeds soon it's going to be too late in the season to plant them.

That's it! I'll tell Aunt Cecelia I forgot I had them, and by the time I remembered, it was well past the suggested planting time.

I still felt uneasy.

"I'm really hungry! What's for breakfast?" Kyle asked, interrupting my thoughts.

"Did you forget?" I asked. "I promised you blueberry pancakes."

Or maybe I should make them with morning glory seeds. That would solve the problem!

"Oh, good! How soon do we eat?"

"Almost ready."

Kyle sat down to wait.

With a bit of flair and a sense of accomplishment, I placed his plate in front of him. The table was already set with the silverware, napkins, and orange juice.

After a quick prayer, Kyle reached for the bottle of syrup, flooded his pancakes, inhaled them, and raced off to play.

I finished eating, gathered the garbage, and headed outside.

Dumping the trash, I turned toward the steps leading to the back door.

"I don't believe it. I ... don't ... believe ... it!"

I stared at the dented white aluminum railing on either side of the cement steps.

"I *do* have a place for those morning glories. I can use the railing!"

The battered railing desperately needed a fresh coat of white paint. But my desire had been to get rid of it rather than to improve its appearance. The railing never had appealed to me. In fact, I hated it.

Suddenly the thought of lush green flowering vines covering that eyesore thrilled me. Two problems solved at once!

Humming my way to the kitchen sink, I filled it with hot water. How pleased I was to have suddenly found the perfect place for the seeds. I wouldn't have to make up any stories for Aunt Cecelia after all.

Grabbing the bottle of dish detergent, I squirted some in the water. *That railing has been there for twenty years. Why didn't I think of it sooner?*

I knew why.

The answer was simple. In my mind the railing was a railing and a problem railing at that. Nothing else. Not a vertical structure for a climbing vine. Just a plain old railing.

But on that particular morning I saw the railing differently and suddenly my unwanted gift had value.

Relishing my new discovery, I began to think about my life. Here I was, a single mother with no job, facing a divorce. One doctor had given me a 2 percent chance to be alive in ten years.

Well, I can't give up, I decided. *I have Kyle to think about. After all, I have found the value of those unwanted morning glory seeds. Maybe I can do the same with some of my painful losses.*

But the mere thought of my circumstances drained my energy.

I turned off the water and decided to rest. I had a lot to think and pray about. I'd do the dishes when I had the strength.

In the years that followed, as God restored my life, I uncovered many gifts in the midst of my undesirable circumstances. As I would not have chosen that packet of morning glory seeds, I never would have chosen all the difficulties in my life. Yet both the seeds and my losses made a positive difference; the seeds transformed my railing, and the troubling times transformed me.

As I share my experiences and those of others, it is important that you understand our stories are God's story. He is able to take the most terrible circumstances and turn them into something positive, but he usually does so one step at a time. These steps are discussed in the following five sections of the book:

Give Yourself Time to Grieve

Investigate and Observe

Find the Value

Take the Risk

Share Your Gifts With Others

Part One

Give Yourself Time to Grieve

Blessed are those who mourn,

for they will be comforted.

MATTHEW 5:4, NIV

Chapter Two

Fallow Fields

"How was I to deal with losing my best friend overnight?" wrote sixteen-year-old Erin in an article for *Brio*, a magazine for teens. "I could have cursed God and shut out the world. I could have become bitter, telling myself no one understood how I felt. But I knew those responses would only make me more lonely and depressed. I decided the wisest thing to do was to grieve...."

Erin's best friend, Liz, had died suddenly from diabetes. "I still long to call Liz and relate my day in its entirety," Erin continued, "or have her do my hair and nails, or page through bridal magazines with her. I wish we could laugh together again, so hard we couldn't breathe, just like we always did. I cry thinking of all our inside jokes and how there won't be any more."[1]

Erin can't escape the void created in her life by Liz's death. Understanding that she needs to take the time to grieve makes her wise beyond her years. As adults, many of us want to struggle and fight with our deep sadness rather than accept it. We think we are weak if we don't quickly bounce back.

Some of us, like Brook who once spoke with me at a women's

retreat, don't even consider grieving. Brook's brother was killed in Vietnam during the '60s.

"My brother and I had been very close, but the expectation I felt from my family was to continue with life as usual. No one ever told me it was necessary to take time to mourn," she said. "Friends told me, 'Keep yourself busy. Time has a way of healing these things.'

"Because I postponed dealing with the loss of my brother, a year after his death I was on the verge of a nervous breakdown. I had to be put on medication."

Ignoring our losses simply doesn't work. Like Brook, either we'll be forced to face our feelings of sadness and anger, or over time our hearts will become hard.

A recent drought helped me to understand the danger of ignoring our feelings. For weeks we had no rain. One scorching day after another left the earth parched until it became as hard as cement. During this same time period, I worked on thinning the irises in my garden. When I first began, the ground was moist, soft, and pliable. But as the hot, dry days continued, the job became more laborious. I could barely dig into the rocklike soil. The hardened earth tightly clenched the irises.

One day, as I attempted to refresh my flowers with water, I knocked over the sprinkling can. The accidental offering of water rolled away, barely being absorbed. The one thing the ground needed was moisture. Yet the once soft earth, now hardened, could not accept it.

Like the parched earth, our hearts harden like cement when the hurts, angers, and losses accumulate. Someone may try to offer a kind word or friendly deed, but we resist it or barely take notice.

What are we to do?

First, we need to recognize the feelings of despair that accompany any significant loss. Then, like Erin, we need to give ourselves permission to grieve.

Unfortunately many of us are more like Heather from Illinois who thought only the most dreadful of tragedies called for sorrow. "I would wrap up any pain or loss I was experiencing, set it on an imaginary scale, and wait to see if a red needle registered that the pain weighed enough," Heather said. "Of course I could always look around and find someone with a loss that was bigger and weighed more than mine, so I never allowed myself to grieve.

"Even though our culture doesn't teach us how to handle grief," Heather continued, "I now know it is a life skill, and my 'pain meter' was a flawed method of coping. I read somewhere the last public American figure to wear a black armband, which signifies a state of mourning, was Franklin Roosevelt. Without this outward symbol our wounds have become invisible."

Although emotional wounds are invisible, they can be as debilitating as any physical illness. We may try to force ourselves to "go on," but it becomes more and more difficult. When our resources are depleted, it is useless to pretend otherwise.

Our lives need to become like a dormant field—seemingly unproductive. Farmers understand the benefit of allowing a field to lie fallow. The soil is revitalized as it accumulates moisture and nutrients. This time of rest and waiting will yield a better harvest in the future. Like the fields lying fallow, our lives are put on hold as we grieve. We must be prepared for the frustration, emptiness, and pain that can accompany what seems like a nonproductive experience.

But when we begin to confront our sorrow and anger, healing begins deep within our soul. We can no more visibly detect this inner healing than we can see the soil of a fallow field being replenished as it rests. Slowly, imperceptibly, our exhausted resources begin to be restored.

How does "fallow" translate in our everyday life? What does it mean to become "fallow"? It means creating the time and space to heal. It means saying no to the little things that crowd out grief. It is not a time to achieve, produce, and perform. Some women choose to erase all but the necessary appointments from their calendar. Others schedule "grief time" to allow space to cry, reflect, or write their thoughts and feelings.

Because I didn't have the physical strength to be involved in the fast-paced world around me, my time of grief occurred along with my slow physical recovery. One of the ways I allowed myself to mourn was by writing my feelings in a journal. I filled up eleven books over five years.

However you carve out your space to heal, like Brook you'll probably encounter the resistance of those who think grieving is a waste of time. They'll say, "Get over it," "Snap out of it," "Get back on your horse and ride again," or, "You need to be doing something besides sitting around and crying."

They consider feeling sad for any length of time as focusing on the negative. Although you may be tempted to think they're right, you must realize they don't understand that healing can't be hurried.

A simple reply might be, "I need time."

"Time for what?" they may ask.

Time to feel. Time to heal.

Time to lie fallow.

Chapter Three

Desert Experience

I'm sorry, but there's nothing else we can do," the doctor said.

I desperately wanted him to prescribe something—anything—to give me back my strength. The transplant, chemotherapy, and radiation had taken their toll on my stamina and endurance.

As the doctor walked out of the room, my desire for a quick recovery walked out with him and hopelessness settled in my heart.

On the ride home, I felt numb. Unaware of my surroundings, I had no idea how to deal with these feelings of loss.

Each day I awoke with an ache in the center of my being, accompanied by the belief that nothing would ever change. Sometimes I would cry; other times I wanted to but couldn't. I forced myself to eat. Winter existed both outdoors and inside of me.

Although I knew depression accompanies grief, I had no clue how intense and debilitating it could be.

"I want to feel lighthearted again. Everything seems so serious and heavy," I said to Lindy, my counselor. "It's like a dark oppressive cloud remains fixed over me. All I do is rest and submit doctor bills, which invariably get rejected by the insurance company for some stupid reason. I realize I can't go back to the way my life was, but the pain I feel..."

"Emotional pain?" Lindy asked.

"Yes, it's far worse than any physical pain I've experienced," I said. "I don't know what to do. I just want this wretched feeling to go away!"

Unfortunately, relief from the suffering that accompanies sorrow doesn't come immediately. Eugene Peterson, author of *The Message*, wrote, "It's arguable that the main difference today is *not* how much people are hurting, but how much they expect to be relieved from their hurting. The previous century suffered just as much—in fact, probably much more.... The big difference today is that we have this mentality that if it's wrong, you can fix it. You don't have to live with any discomfort or frustration."[2]

The incorrect assumption that we shouldn't have to tolerate pain only adds to our misery when our situation doesn't improve. We wonder, "What's wrong with me? Why can't I get rid of this tormenting ache in my soul? Why can't I dust myself off and move on?"

We need to understand that depression is a journey through the desert—a long arduous trek through hot arid terrain. But like the Israelites, who learned to know God in the midst of their desert discomfort, we, too, can experience the living God in the midst of our emotional battles.

In the seventeenth chapter of Exodus we read that the Israelites' spirits were low as they confronted one dilemma after another. They had just solved the problem of no water when the Amalekites attacked (Exodus 17:8-13, NIV)!

Joshua, at Moses' direction, chose some men and prepared for battle. While Joshua and his men were fighting, Moses went to the top of the hill and held up the staff of God. By holding up his hands Moses was symbolically appealing to God for help. "As long as Moses held up his hands, the Israelites were winning, but whenever he lowered his hands, the Amalekites were winning" (Exodus 17:11, NIV).

Holding up a staff for hours can be tough, and Moses' arms grew weary. Aaron and Hur retrieved a stone (symbol of the Lord as our firm foundation) on which Moses could rest, and they held up Moses' hands until Joshua overcame the Amalekite army.

The Israelites' three-step approach can be helpful to us when our spirits are low and we think we can't go on.

Request God's help.

We need to accept our vulnerability, admit *we are helpless*, and, like Moses lifting up his arms in the desert, appeal to God for help.

During radiation treatments, when my blood counts kept dropping to dangerously low levels, my insurance company informed me they had decided not to pay the $105,000 for the bone marrow transplant I had completed several months earlier.

It was during this time that I penned the following in my journal.

February 5, 1990:
At times the ache inside feels like I'm sick—homesick. But I am at home! Maybe it is a yearning for another home, one without pain.

Wherever I go it hurts; the pain follows me. Lord, please help me; only *you* can help.

I will admit that I spent a lot of time mumbling and grumbling and seeking the help of others. However, it was when I acknowledged I was helpless and requested God's guidance that my circumstances and my outlook slowly began to improve.

Although asking for God's help doesn't guarantee instant relief, we must not be like King Asa (2 Chronicles 16:12) who sought help only from physicians and did not seek assistance from God.

Rest and trust in him when you grow weary.

Once during a follow-up visit, while jotting some notes in my file, my doctor looked up at me. "I don't know how you do it," he said. "So much is stacked against you. Not only are you attempting to regain your strength but you've lost your job, your marriage, and now you're in the middle of fighting the insurance company."

I pointed to heaven and replied, "That's the only hope I have."

Perhaps I was learning to rest and trust in God, instead of resisting what life had brought my way.

Rely on help and support from others.

Most of us prefer to give help rather than receive it, but it sometimes becomes necessary to allow others to support us.

Help for my insurance problems came from friends and acquaintances who saw the injustice and were willing to "hold up my arms." It took five years and the involvement of lawyers, but eventually the insurance company did pay for the transplant.

Finding hope in the midst of despair can seem impossible— like searching for beauty in the midst of filth. But when there's *nothing* more you can do, remember the three R's:

1. Request God's help.
2. Rest and trust in him.
3. Rely on others.

Chapter Four

Understanding Our Differences

What do you mean you just want to be left alone?" my best friend asked me. "I feel like you're withdrawing from all your friends. We know things aren't easy for you right now, and we want to help."

My friend and I, however, had two different perceptions of what "help" looked like. As an introvert I yearned for long stretches of time by myself to rest and renew. How could I explain this to my extroverted friend who was energized by people? She was convinced that I needed to be surrounded and entertained by friends to keep my spirits from sagging.

In order for our closest relationships to *help* rather than *hinder* healing, it is necessary to recognize that we don't all grieve or heal in the same ways. Some of us like to be left alone. Others require lots of company. You may prefer to take charge of your problems while your best friend likes to allow things to work out on their own.

Likewise, each plant in my garden has distinctive preferences. My irises, for instance, like to bathe in direct sunlight. Hostas, however, are happiest in filtered sunlight under a tree or shrub.

For my flowers to flourish, I need to provide the conditions that encourage healthy growth.

What do you need when going through difficult times? Although one pat answer is far too simplistic, it is safe to assume that only those people with similar personalities will have the same desires or preferences during adversity.

In their book *Getting Along with Almost Anybody,* Florence and Marita Littauer describe four different personality types and their emotional desires, based on a system originated by Hippocrates and other Greek philosophers.

The Popular Sanguines, like my best friend, are outgoing, fun-loving, and full of energy. Their basic desire in life is to have fun. They like attention, affection, and approval, which can be supplied by lots of visitors, flowers, cards, and calls.

The opposite of the Popular Sanguine is the Perfect Melancholy. This is my personality. Melancholies tend to be meticulous, sensitive, and organized. While the extroverted Sanguine is recharged around people, the introverted Melancholy is energized by solitude. We enjoy silence and space to be alone with our thoughts and emotions. We desire a feeling of warmth and sensitivity in our relationships and are happiest with good doses of well-spaced company rather than a steady stream of guests.

Powerful Cholerics are strong, dynamic, natural-born leaders. Their basic desire is for control. They crave a sense of achievement and accomplishment, as well as appreciation for the challenges they are facing. During troubling times, if they are able, they will work hard to gain an upper hand on the problem. If that approach isn't successful, they will pour themselves into their jobs, start a new project, or exercise harder. When life gets stressful Cholerics like to be provided with choices, such as what to eat or which movie to rent. This helps them to regain a sense of control.

The Peaceful Phlegmatics are the easygoing, likable, balanced people. Emotionally they prefer peace and quiet, and like the Melancholy they are recharged by silence and space. Respect and a feeling of worth for who they are, not what they have done, are important to them. During stressful times, it is not unusual to find the Phlegmatic watching TV, taking a nap, reading, or fishing.[3]

Darlene from New York and her husband, Nelson, frequently fought after the loss of their family business. "She would have as many as forty or fifty friends here in one week," Nelson complained. "There was always a meeting at our house with people coming and going. To me, it was craziness!"

In contrast to his Sanguine wife, Nelson retreated outdoors to be by himself.

When seventeen-year-old Nate Heavilin was killed by a drunk driver, his mother, Marilyn, wrote that her marriage was severely tested before she and her husband understood that they were grieving differently. Marilyn's Melancholy/Choleric personality wanted to make everything right and have control, even if it meant fighting for it. Glen, a Phlegmatic, yearned for peace and hated the conflicts brought on by the insurance company and a manslaughter trial.

"Glen didn't look like a peacemaker to me anymore," Marilyn says. "He looked like Mr. Milque Toast. I wanted him to protect me from the cold, cruel world and make people be nice to me. Instead, he kept telling me I should be patient."[4]

When Marilyn realized that each personality has distinctive goals, she said, "Glen was not responding differently from me just to buck me, and he wasn't necessarily saying I was wrong.

We simply were looking at the world through different eyes."[5]

Whatever our personality, we alleviate much of the tension in our relationships during adversity by giving ourselves permission *to grieve in our own way* and allowing others to grieve in theirs.

"The grass is always greener on the other side of the fence" is a familiar expression. My experience in gardening, however, leads me to believe that the grass is usually greenest when it is given what it needs, whether that be water, lime, nitrogen, or sunlight.

Do you prefer moments of lighthearted distraction in the midst of your problems and pain or quiet moments to be alone and sort through things? Do you want a chance to work more or exercise longer? Or do you prefer the opportunity to withdraw from life and rest?

When adversity strikes, remember our responses to tragedy are not the same. Like my best friend and I discovered, this understanding can be the difference between hurting and healing.

Chapter Five

When Nothing Seems to Change

I t's been long enough already! I want this all to be history," Tracey from Missouri said with a tone of disgust after months of dealing with her son's drug abuse. "It's the sameness I hate— day after day, week after week, the same problems, the same obstacles. It feels like things will *never* get better."

Like Tracey, I remember awakening each day with the belief that nothing would ever change. Pulling the covers over my head and hiding in the comfort of my bed seemed like the best solution to my problems.

It didn't take long for me to realize, however, that I would stay stuck in the muck of despair if I didn't adopt a more positive approach. Because I could only handle the emotional pain in small doses, I learned to alternate activities that provided some sense of relief or enjoyment with time to confront my problems and the heart-wrenching ache within.

Other women, like Debbie, whom I met at a writers' conference, also discovered that dealing with their pain a little bit at a time was the most helpful approach.

Debbie's thirty-one-year-old husband died of cancer, leaving her to raise their two young daughters alone. "I feel like a big bottle of soda that has been shaken," she told me. "God allows me to open the lid a little bit at a time and then close it. But God forbid if I'd open it all at once. It would be a big explosion!" Healthy outlets for Debbie were being with friends and going to the ocean with her family.

Gardening, walking, writing in my journal, visiting with a friend, or watching a movie were a few of the activities that kept me from going over the edge.

As my stamina increased and I was able to travel, vacations gave me a chance to see another world and escape from mine. No matter how brief, they broke the cycle of feeling overwhelmed and gave me an extra boost to continue my climb out of the pit of despair.

As a divorced, single mom, Joanne had limited opportunity to get away for any length of time. I was speaking in Maryland when she shared with me how she solved her problem. "I'd take one-day retreats at a nearby convent," she said. "I'd listen to tapes, write in my journal, walk, or even sleep. It was so restoring without the children or the phone demanding my attention.

"I also enjoyed taking short trips to Goodwill and consignment shops to treasure hunt," she continued. "God provided me with many little gifts and surprises during these excursions. I went home renewed and recharged."

Renea, an airline stewardess from Minnesota, suffered serious head injuries when hit by a falling piece of freight. She found making a "God bag" invaluable. "I would write each of my problems on a piece of paper and put them in my God bag. It was a visual reminder of my intention to give them to the Lord," she said. "Whenever I accomplished a difficult task in my physical therapy, I splurged on a bouquet of balloons to keep my spirits up. And, believe it or not, I actually sent myself incredibly beautiful cards."

Gardening was one of the activities that enabled Ida Rose from Pennsylvania to get through the dark dreary days after her diagnosis of cancer. Knowing I was a gardener, Ida Rose told me, "God spoke to me so powerfully when I got in the dirt and watched things grow. Seeing the miracle of a seed becoming a plant and the plant becoming a vegetable on my dinner table helped me believe God could change things in my life and heal me.

"Arranging pictures of my family in a scrapbook also helped," Ida Rose said. "These pictures were reminders of God's miracles in my life. I had been told I would never have children. For seven years I went through infertility treatments but didn't get pregnant. Then, unexpectedly, God blessed us with three children. Later, during my cancer treatments, as I placed the pictures of the children I was told I'd never have in my book, I found myself focusing again on God's miracles. All the things I had hoped for during those years of infertility had come true."

It is easy to slip into the mind-set that the sun will never shine again when one dreary day seems to follow another. But instead of wallowing in our hurts, we must take an active approach and plan activities that will provide us with reminders of hope and a sense of relief.

As the following journal entries show, alternating a favorite activity with time to feel the pain made all the difference for me.

April 19, 1990
This is a quiet and private desperation. If you ever wrote a

detailed account of going through depression, no one would read it. The book would be slow, long, drawn out, heavy, monotonous. Everyone wants to offer his or her quick solution. For grief there is none. The process is overwhelming, like chopping down a forest with a dull ax.

The next day after going to my garden and collecting a lovely bouquet of lavender tulips, I made this entry:

April 20, 1990
Beauty and hope are growing in my garden. For just as the tulips bloom in the spring, one day joy will return to my life.

And one day it did.

Chapter Six

Seeing Red

Have you ever felt angry and fed up with everyone and everything? I have and often wondered if that is how a murderer feels. It's a scary, crazy, horrible feeling.

Although I had expected the deep sadness I felt over the loss of my health, job, and marriage, what I didn't anticipate was the seething rage.

The first couple of years after my cancer treatments and divorce, *any* event, however insignificant, that was beyond my control could trigger the fury I had held within during the countless medical procedures and legal issues. To my dismay, my son was often the recipient of this unleashed rage.

I remember exploding the day I gave Kyle a lesson on how to wash my car properly.

"Overlap your strokes as you wash," I said as I demonstrated the procedure on the driver's side door. "Like this."

My eleven-year-old son, who had washed the car numerous times, wiped here and there. The untouched areas of grime annoyed me.

"Please keep your strokes close together," I calmly repeated, although I was starting to simmer.

He ignored me and swiped his sponge wherever he pleased.

Exasperated, I yelled, "Kyle, look what you're doing!"

Our tug-of-war quickly escalated. Boiling with rage, I picked up the bucket of dirty water and dumped it on him.

Dripping with water and justified annoyance, Kyle looked at me and hollered, "Mom! This is ridiculous."

He was right. I quickly apologized and stomped off before I regretted another word or deed.

Anger, like depression, is very much a part of grief. Giving full vent to our anger, however, only makes things worse.

Sallie, whom I met while speaking in Alabama, also struggled with rage. When her twenty-year-old son died in a car accident, she prayed that she could mourn the way God designed. But she never expected what surfaced about a year and a half after her son's death as she wallpapered a bathroom.

"Like a slow leak in a dam, tiny words of anger trickled into my thoughts until they formed gushing statements of rage. I began to yell and scream at God. 'Where were you? Why did you let Wes die? Why do I have to hurt so badly?' On and on I yelled. Shocking even myself, I picked up an unwrapped roll of wallpaper and hit a book.

"Then I did the unthinkable. I knocked my Bible across the room. I was challenging God. I was crossing a line. He was holy and mighty and could have wiped me out with one single word. But he didn't. He waited and listened silently. His silence was not one of rejection, scorn, or disapproval. His expression was clear, strong, and loving. And he let me fight him.

"I fought and fought knowing who would win, but I was so angry I didn't care. I cried out to God for deliverance from my grief until I was exhausted, sleepy, and numb. And as only a loving, patient heavenly Father can do, he spoke with words of grace and truth and said, 'I knew all along what was in your heart. I just wanted you to see it.'

"That was when I knew everything was OK," she continued. "God had seen my anger and watched me empty it at his feet. I began to understand the depth of his fatherly love a little better, and I fell into his arms and wept."

In order to avoid the destruction that can result from rage held within, we must acknowledge the anger that comes with loss. Then we can work toward recycling it into something positive and godly. Otherwise it may be expressed in ways we regret. Just ask Kyle.

Here are a few suggestions for recycling our anger:

Do something physical.

Furious that her husband had left her and their three children for his young secretary, Carolyn said, "Exercise and gardening became a release for my rage. I worked out almost every morning, and in the evening after dinner I ranted, raved, fussed, and fumed as I weeded my garden."

I, too, recycled my anger in the garden. One morning after battling the insurance company over the bill for my transplant, I headed for my backyard.

The weeds became insurance agents. "You don't care about people!" I yanked out a skunk cabbage. "You only care about money!" I uprooted a dandelion. "When people need insurance, you don't pay." I dug at the roots of a thistle. "You only want to take care of healthy people."

The physical exertion helped me vent my fury. But it didn't happen overnight. Like the weeds that have a persistent way of reappearing, so did my anger. I had to continue processing it.

Any activity that expends physical energy such as cleaning the house, kneading dough, pounding nails, or digging in the dirt can help us dispel our wrath.

Pray, reflect, and meditate.
We can begin praying for eyes to see, ears to hear, and a heart to perceive God's perspective for those circumstances that upset us. "Lord, how do you want me to respond to this?" or "How do you want me to see this?" are questions I have often asked.

Dr. Mark Futato, Professor of Old Testament at Reformed Theological Seminary in Orlando, Florida, once told me, "Through the Book of Psalms, God gives us the freedom to ask our agonizing questions in prayer, questions like 'Where were you?' and 'Why?' For example, 'Why, O Lord, do you stand far off? Why do you hide yourself in times of trouble?' (Psalm 10:1, NIV); 'My God, my God, why have you forsaken me? Why are you so far from saving me, so far from the words of my groaning?'" (Psalm 22:1, NIV).

Write in a journal.
Our journals can be a safe place to unload toxic thoughts. As we write we begin to shed our deep hurts and irritations.

My journal entry on September 26, 1992:

I find myself so angry, hurt, irritated, and furious. I will write down every little thing that is annoying me and give the list to Jesus. I will ask him to take it and make something good of it.

1. I'm angry at all the things to do around the house. The cooking, cleaning, bills, ironing, clothes to wash and mend.
2. I'm angry with Kyle. All he wants to do is play Nintendo

or watch TV and then do his homework at the last minute.

3. I'm angry at my lack of stamina and energy.
4. I'm angry that all I seem to do is go to doctor appointments.

Share your feelings.

Whether we talk to a counselor or caring friend, a good listener can help us express our aggravations constructively.

"Some days the urge to destroy frightens me. I'm afraid that by expressing my anger I'll lose control and be hauled away in a straightjacket," I told Lindy, my counselor.

"Don't forget: acknowledging your rage is a healthy sign and as much a part of grief as sadness," Lindy reminded me.

"It doesn't feel healthy," I responded. "It feels awful."

Get rest, eat well, and set priorities.

If every little thing annoys me, it's time for some rest and pampering.

"It's amazing how much smaller my problems appeared after a good dinner and a good night's sleep," a friend told me. She was discovering that taking time to rest and renew after a difficult week enabled her to release her frustrations and focus on what really mattered.

Ephesians 4:26(NRSV) reminds us, "Be angry but do not sin."

Rather than being afraid when anger grips us, we ought to tremble at the thought of *what will happen if we lash out rather than face our fury.*

Expressing our aggravation is a bit like taking out the trash. Our anger, irritations, and frustrations need to be discarded or recycled. Just be careful where they're dumped.

Chapter Seven

Black Gold

E ven though no one saw me, I was embarrassed by the tears
flowing down my cheeks. After all, it was such a silly thing.

Only one week earlier an exquisite arrangement of home-
grown purple delphiniums and white snapdragons had dec-
orated my kitchen table. They made me feel like a princess. I
wanted those flowers to last longer. I wanted to save them
somehow.

As I added the limp petals and wilted leaves to my compost
pile, I stared at the once vibrant bouquet. Like so many things
in my life that had been lovely, these flowers were now dead—
gone forever.

It's funny how an insignificant event, such as a lifeless bouquet, could trigger more heartache. Like so many times before,
I again found myself wondering if I would *ever* get over the
devastating feelings of loss.

I pondered the compost pile before me. Dead plant material
had been mixed with soil and water. Pine needles, fruit and vegetable scraps, grass clippings, fallen leaves, dead flowers, and
plants lay rotting in a heap.

This pile of debris wouldn't decompose overnight. Heat and

time would eventually break it down into rich dark humus or, in gardener's language, black gold.

Because compost contains a wealth of nutrients and antibiotics, a garden can never have too much of it. When mixed with plantings, the black gold insures larger, healthier, more abundant flowers and vegetables.

Often on hot summer days when I lift the black rubber covering to add my latest castoffs to the pile, the stench catches my breath. The decomposing matter not only has a strong odor but is not a pretty sight—a steamy slimy mess.

When we are in the midst of grieving, it's easy to doubt that anything good could come out of devastation. In the Old Testament, Isaiah comforts and encourages those who mourn in Israel by telling them that the Lord will give "beauty for ashes"(Isaiah 61:3, LB). During my time of mourning, I often wondered how my ashes would ever be made beautiful.

However, as I watched the mound of dead plant material slowly being transformed into rich compost, I began to understand how my accumulated losses could become fertilizer to promote new growth and beauty.

One of my close friends, Suzanne, also remembers her uncertainty about how her losses could turn into something lovely.

"I never had any children of my own," Suzanne said, "and so when I married I was naïve but thrilled to have the privilege of helping my husband raise his son and daughter. For years it seemed all was well and our new family was growing closer. Then our son, William, turned sixteen. His suddenly rebellious attitude not only affected my relations with him but my marriage as well.

"Although William demolished two new cars in a short time, my husband saw to it that our son always had another new one. Whether it was the school calling to report William's unexcused absence or the police informing us of his drunk driving, my husband always had an excuse for William's irresponsible behavior.

"Because I felt our son should suffer the consequences of his behavior, I discovered two of my most precious relationships crumbling apart. To William, I was no longer Mom but 'that woman.' To my husband, Dan, I was no longer a wife and mother to his children but a depressed woman he didn't know.

"Suicidal feelings overwhelmed me. I couldn't see any reason to go on living. Finally I sought the help of a psychologist, who gradually assisted me in working through my anger and despair.

"It took two years, but little by little I felt better about myself and believed my friends when they told me I was 'a woman of value.'

"That was a year ago. Today not only has William matured but he is successfully employed in another state. I thank God that we are now very good friends. My relationship with my husband has also been enriched. He no longer views me as a depressed, nagging wife but as someone very special.

"Looking back it was my relationship with God, my friends, and the psychologist that gave me hope to continue. God took all that was lost and used it to transform my life. Although at times it would have been easier to walk away, my husband, son, and I worked through our hurts and pains, one step at a time, each one of us growing and maturing."

If, like Suzanne, you, too, find hope slipping away, remember the compost pile and its gradual transformation from garbage to gold. Our accumulated losses become the substance for new growth. We take that which has died and place it on God's compost pile to break down and rot.

Whether it takes months or years, our grief decomposes into rich nourishing soil for a new life. But until that happens, like the compost pile, grief is not a pretty sight, and it stinks!

Chapter Eight

Even the Flowers Experience Dark Times

Over the years I've asked women who have experienced tragic loss to complete an informal survey. One of the questions asks, "Did grieving take more or less time than you expected?"

The vast majority responds, "More." Some volunteer, "Much more!"

"Grieving takes longer than anybody ever has the patience for," Dr. Elizabeth Palazzi, a Pennsylvania licensed psychologist, told me. "People don't always talk about how long it takes to grieve and heal after a painful situation."

Our society wants to apply our high-tech, microwave mentality to our physical, emotional, and spiritual healing. However, grief cannot be hurried.

Our lack of understanding only adds to the heartache for those already suffering. Job reflected this when he said, "And now their sons mock me in song; I have become a byword among them. They detest me and keep their distance; they do not hesitate to spit in my face" (Job 30:9-10, NIV).

Like Job, the words of Brook's friends created more pain for her. We met Brook in chapter two when she talked about the loss of her brother in Vietnam. Years later, after one of Brook's sons died from the complications of AIDS, a friend said, "Your son died three years ago; shouldn't you be over this by now?"

But Brook still found herself bursting into hysterical sobs over the least little thing. For example, one day while she folded a basket of towels, her husband said, "Someone backed into Joe and Alice's new lawnmower; it's ruined. You should see it. Boy, are they upset!"

"Well!" shrieked Brook, shocking them both as she tossed the laundry in the air. "How would they like to have lost a son—how would that feel?"

With the laundry scattered around them, her husband held and rocked her until she could cry no longer.

"People often say to those who are hurting, 'Aren't you over this yet?' It would be much kinder and closer to the truth," Dr. Palazzi suggests, "if we would say, 'I don't know what you're going through,' or, 'I wish I could help you but I can't.'"

Adding to the length of time needed to grieve is the fact that we often relive the terror or pain of our loss. This happened one day as I was having a routine blood test. Because there is a great deal of scar tissue in my veins as a result of chemotherapy, it takes someone with experience to get blood on the first try. On this day, however, I got a student nurse who had to stick me four times with the needle before getting any blood. Nothing could have prepared me for the panic that followed.

I felt as though I were right back in the midst of my bone marrow transplant. The smell of alcohol and the repeated stabs of the needle triggered thoughts of lying helplessly in the hospital bed with a fever, not knowing if I was going to live. I started to tremble inside. My heart pounded fiercely. My head began to spin as my mind raced. I felt nauseated. I thought I was suffocating.

"I've got to get out of this hospital and get some fresh air, away from this smell," I thought. "I feel like I'm going crazy. I hate blood tests. I just hate them!"

I left the room, ready to explode, and kicked a wall in the hallway. Tears streamed down my face as I hurried toward the exit. I wanted to be in my car; I would feel safe there.

It's natural for both the people dealing with the difficult times and for those who love them to become impatient when healing takes longer than they expect.

Recognizing that everyone involved wants the problems to be over helps to reduce misunderstandings.

In Psalm 13, David echoes the feelings and questions of those who have had to endure seemingly endless suffering. "How long, O Lord? Will you forget me forever? How long will you hide your face from me? How long must I wrestle with my thoughts and every day have sorrow in my heart?" (Psalm 13:1-2, NIV).

Eventually, our time of weeping and mourning does come to an end. We know in the depths of our soul that we have accepted to some degree "what is."

"The sharpness of the pain—the feeling of desperateness—passes," Brook said, "but there is a part of grief that is everlasting."

I once heard Sammy Lou Johnston from Mississippi say in a speech, "When you see a pretty flower remember God brought it through a lot of dirt." Like the soil, which is a growing medium for plants, sorrow and time are the dirt that provides us with the environment in which to grieve and grow.

Certain plants like the poinsettia require a period of darkness in order to bloom. It is often in the blackness of our grief that optimum conditions are met, so that our resources are replenished and we can blossom once more.

If those around you don't understand how long the struggles and pain can last, remember that God brings some of the most exquisite flowers through dirt and dark times. But it doesn't happen overnight.

Chapter Nine

After Winter Comes Spring

The importance of making room for new life came to me early one spring as I cleared my garden of the rotting remains of dead plants and leaves. In one area, hidden underneath the decaying matter, I found small bright green stalks of daffodils. The tip of one stalk had actually broken through several layers of debris in an effort to reach the light. Nearby was a group of daffodils whose stems were twice as tall and well on their way to forming buds. This second cluster of bulbs had not been hampered by any rotting debris. Although both groups were doing the best they could under the circumstances, this experience reminded me that rotting debris can stunt growth. I began to wonder what new growth I was hindering because I hadn't cleared out the old.

Patsy Clairmont reflects this same thought in *Under His Wings.* "None of us gets through this life without experiencing loss—of loved ones (through distance, divorce, and death), income, reputation, home, innocence, and so on. But many of us harbor our losses and therefore our grief, leaving us little room for joy or other life-giving qualities."[6]

Leslie, whom I met in Texas, recognized she had to force herself to make the decision to let go and move on after her daughter's murder. "While I watched an old TV Western, a cowboy said, 'Some people bury their dead and some people let their dead bury them.' I realized I was allowing my loss to 'bury' me," Leslie said. "Melinda's memory would be better served by allowing something beautiful, rather than something ugly, to come out of her life and death."

Leslie's right. Holding on to losses hampers new beginnings. Joan Lunden, a former cohost of *Good Morning America,* said following her divorce, "Holding on to anger, resentment and hurt only gives you tense muscles, a headache and a sore jaw from clenching your teeth. Forgiveness gives you back the laughter and the lightness in your life."[7]

As we forgive, we release "what could have been" and accept "what is." But that's easier said than done. When I think how I want to hold on to simple things like delicate pink cherry blossoms, that I don't want them to drop from the tree, why should I be surprised at the struggle I face to give up something I so desperately wanted that can never be?

Yet, as we let go of the small things and watch something new appear, we can learn to accept the bigger losses.

A journal entry from March 25, 1994:

I was mesmerized by tonight's sunset. As I inhaled the unbelievable beauty of the sky, I began to wonder if I could describe it in words. There were long horizontal brush strokes the color of crimson with cottony streaks in shades of light red and pink, richly painted on a gray sky with accents of navy. The stark black silhouettes of the trees against this display created an artistic urge within me.

How could I preserve this beauty on canvas or with a camera?

But neither would capture the brilliance, the vastness of the sky. As I contemplated how to hold on to it forever, the image vanished into darkness. Yet, the picture remained in my memory with feelings of awe, peace, and joy.

Why do I want to hold on to all that was lovely? Why do I think the canvas will never again be so brilliant? Lord, help me to accept the beauty or sadness of each moment and yield to the inevitable changes of life.

Our tendency is to want to capture and save what was important to us, but, like a lovely sunset or a delicate flower, the important things in life can't be locked up and held forever. We need to trust that one day our Lord will replace our mourning with gladness and give us joy instead of sorrow (Jeremiah 31:13).

In the meantime, we must clear out the old, even if we have nothing growing in its place.

Grief, like winter, is only a season. And after every winter comes spring, a time of new beginnings and fresh starts. When we give ourselves time to grieve and let go of what no longer can be, then we are ready to grow anew, like the yellow daffodils of springtime.

Reflection From the Garden

If you have never made a compost pile, you may want to try it. Watching the debris decay is fascinating, and the compost will do wonders for your garden. First, choose a sunny spot that is not visible from the main part of your backyard but within easy access. My pile is behind a row of pine trees.

Then decide what kind of container you will use. There are many types of compost containers on the market, but I used cement blocks, stacked about three feet high in the shape of a *U*. Placing the blocks on their side adds extra ventilation through the cores.

Next, mix some soil with grass clippings, vegetable and fruit scraps, dead plants that are not diseased, and fallen leaves. After it rains and becomes very wet, cover the pile with heavy black rubber or plastic. This attracts the heat, holds in the moisture, and speeds up the decomposing. If you don't want to wait for the rain, wet your mixture with a garden hose.

The first year I mixed my "black gold" (compost) with some annuals in only one area of my garden to see if the rich humus made any difference. At the end of the summer a young neighbor boy who occasionally helped me remarked, "Wow! Look how much bigger and healthier those flowers are. You need to make lots of compost."

Although one pile is enough for me to maintain, he was right; there was a noticeable difference. Now every time I add something to my compost pile I am reminded of how God uses the dead stuff in my life as fertilizer to promote healthy new growth.

Part Two

Investigate and Observe

Give me eyes to see, ears to hear,

and a heart to perceive thy will.

PRAYER BASED ON ACTS 28:27

Chapter Ten

Empty Basket

A re you aware there's nothing in your basket?" a young
businessman asked. He was already settled into his first-
class seat. I stood waiting in the aisle to reach mine located in
the back of the plane.

"Yes," I replied smiling, then blushed as I glanced around.
His comment had attracted the attention of everyone near me.
All eyes focused on my empty basket.

I guess I did look pretty silly. The basket, filled with bright-
colored shredded paper, was wrapped in clear cellophane and
topped with a large hot pink bow. It looked as if it was ready to
be presented to someone, except for the obvious fact that its
contents were missing. A plain empty basket would not have
attracted such attention.

The man's continued staring begged the question, *Why
would you bother to carry an empty basket?*

An explanation seemed necessary.

"I'm planning to use it at a garden retreat I'm having. It will
be filled with twenty pairs of canvas gloves, and the cellophane
will keep them from falling out. We're stenciling the gloves with
morning glories."

That seemed to satisfy the man, and he returned to his newspaper.

Finally, I arrived at my seat only to discover that the basket was too large to fit into the overhead bin. I had no choice but to sacrifice my legroom and wedge the parcel underneath the seat in front of me.

The people seated across the aisle watched the whole process.

"May I ask why you're bothering with an empty basket?" one of them asked with a friendly smile.

"It's a large sturdy basket," I explained, "and I want to use it for an upcoming event. I received it at a hospital where I just spoke," I continued. "It was filled with fruit, bottled water, and crackers. I used them but was careful to preserve the cellophane."

"You could always buy another one," the lady suggested. "I'm not sure I'd haul that across the country."

I considered the basket worth the effort. It had possibilities, and I had a purpose for it.

But, after the third trip to an airport bathroom during stopovers, I, too, began to wonder. On each visit I struggled to get the basket, my overnight bag, and my pocketbook inside the stall with me.

I guess I should have anticipated the inconvenience, but I didn't expect an empty basket to arouse such curiosity.

Adversity sometimes gives us empty baskets to lug around. Often we don't know what our basket or new life will hold, but in the meantime, we have the burden of hauling it from place to place.

Our natural tendency, like that of the young businessman and lady across the aisle, is to focus on the fact that our basket is empty. But we can choose to concentrate on what we do have, even if it is only an empty basket filled with possibilities.

During my treatments for cancer, it was easy for me to glance in the mirror and notice my bald head and the dark circles under my eyes. Yet I needed to consider more than the obvious fact that my life was threatened. I needed to look for the positive aspects of my illness.

"If I were facing the possible end of my life, I don't think I could find any gifts in that situation," one lady said to me. However, as Theodore Roethke wrote, "In a dark time, the eye begins to see."[8]

When our lives are turned upside down through major losses, we begin to "see" things differently.

For instance, how many of us have perceived physical attractiveness to be a handicap? Golda Meir, former Prime Minister of Israel, did.

"Not being beautiful was the true blessing," she said. "Not being beautiful forced me to develop my inner resources. The pretty girl has a handicap to overcome."[9]

Like Golda Meir, we need to view our limitations as assets. It didn't take me long to realize that cancer provided me with the opportunity to savor the time I did have and use it to grow stronger in my faith.

You may, because of your circumstances, find that life has left you carrying an empty basket. If so, remember that it may appear empty but actually it contains endless possibilities.

Chapter Eleven

Dead Flowers— Seeds for a New Life

"My grandfather and his six brothers built this church, and I am not leaving!" Grandpa said as he crossed his arms and dug in his heels. My grandpa, Earl Hoover, Sr., was not one to change his mind.

The church where I grew up was known as Hoover's Church for nearly a century. It consisted of two congregations, Lutheran and Dutch Reformed. The original charter of 1844 stated that services were to be in the German language and the church was to used by the Lutherans, Reformed, and Mennonites of the area.

Each week during my childhood, the Lutheran and Dutch Reformed congregations alternated worship services (in English). After a time, the Dutch Reformed congregation, to which my family belonged, grew in size and began a building fund to erect their own church so they could have services every Sunday.

One afternoon, Reverend Henning, the young minister of our congregation, came to visit Grandpa. After some small talk, he addressed the topic of breaking up the merged congregations.

"I'm not leaving this church," Grandpa said firmly.

"I know the thought of leaving what your grandfather and his brothers built isn't easy," Reverend Henning said. "You have lots of history and memories there. It even holds your family name. But just think, if you help us build this new church, *your grandchildren* will be able to say, 'My grandpa built this church.'"

Grandpa stared at the floor saying nothing. Then he stood up, walked to his desk, and wrote a check to the building fund.

In the fall of 1959, the new church was dedicated. Today, I can proudly say that both my grandpa and my great-great-grandfather were instrumental in building two churches.

However, if Grandpa had not been open-minded enough to reconsider his position, I wouldn't be able to make this statement. Grandpa shifted his focus from the past and what his grandfather had done to the future and what he could do for his grandchildren.

Like Grandpa, I can get stuck in the past and refuse to look for new opportunities. Every fall when my bright-colored flowers fade and shrivel, I get melancholy. Ignoring the crisp blue skies and autumn hues, I see only that my flowers are dying.

I especially pouted the very first year of my new garden. But one fall afternoon as a friend and I collected the brown dried zinnias, she said, "Just imagine, these withered blossoms contain the substance for new life, the seeds for future bouquets. You're already beginning next summer's garden."

"I never thought of it that way," I said.

Haven't we all experienced times when our narrow view of a situation caused problems? In my family this tendency seems to get passed on with each generation. When my son was a senior in high school, he said, "Mom, I'm quitting swimming."

"What?" I sputtered, appalled.

Kyle had been the state butterfly champion in tenth grade and had been offered a full scholarship to swim at college.

"Let's think about this some more."

But Kyle crossed his arms, dug in his heels, and stated, "Since I was sick last year, my ranking has dropped a lot, and I'm tired of the agony of working toward a comeback. It's just too hard and painful. I'd be much happier if I would quit for good. I'll *never* be able to swim like I did before."

That night I prayed for wisdom.

The next morning at breakfast I said, "Kyle, remember the story of Grandpa Hoover, how he kept focusing on the past and what his grandfather had done?"

"Yeah, I remember."

"Well, the young minister helped Grandpa to look at the situation differently. Isn't there any other way you could look at what's happening in your life?"

"I don't know," Kyle mumbled.

"Well, you want to be a swim coach after college, and you're certainly going to have swimmers who feel just like you do right now, swimmers who think they have no other choice but to quit."

Kyle was silent.

"If you can stick with it and learn how to get past this," I continued, "you'll be an awesome coach someday. Your swimmers will listen to you because they'll know you've been there."

Did it work? Does a parent of a teenager ever know? But Kyle's still swimming—in college.

Maybe years from now when my future granddaughter is entangled in a problem, stubbornly refusing to change her mind, Kyle will say, "Remember the story of Grandpa Hoover, how he ..."

Chapter Twelve

When It Rains, It Pours

"If my lawn looked like that, I'd shoot myself!" a neighbor said, pointing to my yard.

While he prided himself on the fairway turf surrounding his home, my lawn resembled a field of Shredded Wheat, brown, stubbly, and strawlike. It was just one more frustration in my life.

"Why would I shoot *myself?*" I asked as we stared at my disaster zone. "I'd like to shoot everyone else!"

Shortly after that comment, he decided he needed to get home.

We had suffered a devastating drought the previous year. Except for a few shaded areas, my lawn had dried up. I assumed that when the spring rains came, my green grass would return.

Spring came, and so did the rains. Everyone's lawn revived except mine. Huge blotches of dead grass, interspersed with a few patches of green turf, replaced what was once a lush lawn.

"Oh, Lord, now what am I going to do?" I wondered.

The estimates I obtained from lawn care services were not encouraging.

"I'd have to charge you two thousand for this job," one man quoted.

"You've got quite a mess here, young lady," another land-scaper said. "The entire lawn needs to be redone. I would have to remove the sod, loosen the soil, and reseed the yard. My fee is going to be around three thousand dollars."

This was all far too expensive for my bank account.

"God, please help me," I pleaded. "What am I to do with this mess?"

Two weeks later, as I again sat on the back steps surveying the pitiful-looking yard, God's answer came.

"I want you to turn it into a lovely flower garden and pond."

A garden? This can't be God's voice I'm hearing.

I thought of my limited resources.

A garden and pond? Surely I must have heard the wrong voice. Isn't that being frivolous? Why a garden?

But throughout the next week, I continued to hear that still small voice gently encouraging me to replace the dead grass with a garden. Like Moses, who was told to take the Israelites out of Egypt, I finally asked, "God, how can I possibly do that? I don't have the strength."

There was no immediate answer so when a friend stopped by the next day, I decided to test the waters.

"I'm so disgusted with this lawn, I've been thinking about turning it into a garden," I told her.

"Great idea!" she replied. "I'll help you."

"Really?" I asked with excitement and disbelief. "You're sure you want to do that?"

"I'd love to! I'm not much of a gardener, but we'll have fun."

During the months that followed, not only did she lend a helping hand but so did many others. One neighbor rototilled the lawn. Jonathan, a ten-year-old neighbor, hauled away buckets of dead sod and rocks, then raked the loose ground smooth.

Another friend, temporarily unemployed, dug a hole for the water. And still another, who happened to manage a nursery, oversaw the laying of the stones around the pond.

Then Jonathan returned to tuck in dozens of summer annuals we found at a clearance sale.

All this time, I sat on the cement steps, offering my opinions and watching the transformation, which for me was difficult. How I yearned to have the strength to do it all myself.

Finally, around the middle of July, the work was finished. God brought the rains that hadn't come the year before, and within a month I had the beginning of a colorful flower garden.

Looking back, I can now see God's plan. Today I have an exquisite, well-established garden where there was once a dead lawn. Mourning Glory Gardens is a living memorial of what God can do with the destruction in our lives. He takes every loss that hurts or makes us angry and turns it into something beautiful.

Chapter Thirteen

 Buttercup Shells

W here did you find all those buttercup shells?" asked a lady walking along the shore.

"Right here on Sanibel Beach," I said. "That's all I'm hunting today. What are you looking for?"

"Oh," she shrugged, "nothing in particular. Just going down the beach about a mile. I wouldn't mind finding all those buttercups, though, like you did."

I reached into my netted bag and pulled out one of the clam-like semitransparent shells. "Here's one to get you started."

"Oh! Thank you." She smiled and held up the orangish yellow shell to the bright sunlight. "It's easy to understand how it got its name."

"There are quite a few here once you zero in on them," I said.

"Guess I better get busy." She hurried off in the opposite direction.

As I combed the beach I thought about her comment about not looking for anything in particular.

In contrast to her, I had headed off to the beach with the fixed goal of collecting buttercups. I wanted to fill a glass jar with them.

Picturing the buttercup shell in my mind, I slowly walked with my head down scanning the shells (clam, conch, moon, turkey wings, and various others) that had washed ashore. Whenever I found a large pile, I carefully sifted through them. If I happened to find a perfect conch shell, I tossed it in my bag. However, my mission that day was to collect buttercups.

It became a game. Some were partially buried in the sand while others were tucked under the debris of broken shells. Some lay with their orangish yellow side up, filled with sandy water, while others were face down resembling an ordinary clam shell. Very few were in plain view to be spotted easily.

When my shell bag was half full, I headed back to the condominium to join my mother and brother. Since I no longer was focused on hunting shells, I saw that the beach was full of people "searching." Most, like the lady I had met, were casually walking, scouting here and there for the conspicuous shell. Several appeared to be serious collectors, stooped down, digging in the sand, pulling up partially buried treasures.

It was apparent from the fullness of shell bags that those who were searching superficially weren't nearly as successful as those concentrating on the task.

This same principle holds true when we seek treasures in our tragedies. Until we get serious and make the commitment to look for specific gifts, either buried or hidden, in our situation, we probably won't uncover much. We need to dig through the rubble of our losses, searching for the value. Like finding the buttercups, very few of our gifts will be lying in plain view.

Years ago, when I was in my twenties, I lived in a mobile home. We had just moved out when a tornado picked up and demolished the trailer, leaving us with a heap of rubble. For weeks, we rummaged through the pile, committed to salvaging anything of value. For everything we uncovered, we asked the same question, "Does it have any worth?" Some items needed repair, while others came through unscathed. We were able to use the latter in other capacities, such as some of the intact kitchen cabinets, which ended up in my mother's cabin.

Just remember that in searching, we tend to stumble upon that which we set out to discover. Do you want to collect buttercups? Then make that your goal. Do you want to find treasures in the midst of your difficulties? Make that your priority. If you hunt for nothing in particular, chances are you'll uncover nothing in particular. Purposeful searching leads to discovery. What is it you're seeking?

Chapter Fourteen

 The Treasures of Darkness

It was 5:00 A.M., and the rays of my flashlight revealed one lovely specimen after another. Low tide and a deserted beach made this a shell collector's dream. With the receding of the sea, many treasures lay waiting to be collected.

But I felt a bit uneasy.

The silent darkness coupled with a chill in the air gave me an eerie feeling. No moon was shining, and there were no lights in the nearby houses. Other than the flashlight's beam, I was wrapped in a blanket of black. Without the lure of the hunt, I would have stayed inside in safety, warmth, and comfort.

"Having any luck?" A man's deep voice from behind startled me.

"Ahhh ... yeah."

I prayed he was a friendly tourist.

"What about you?" I asked, steadying my voice.

"No flashlight. Makes it tough to see. I'll know when I get to my room if I picked up anything worthwhile."

He quickened his pace as he strode past me.

As his sandals scrunched the sand, I was both relieved and disappointed, relieved that he meant no harm and disappointed that I was not really the first on the beach.

My disappointment soon faded, though, as I continued to retrieve some real beauties. These treasures seemed even more valuable because I knew someone else had skipped right over them.

A few minutes later, I spied a faint light coming toward me. It was moving back and forth, scanning the edge of the water—another shell seeker.

"Good morning! Great shelling, isn't it?" the approaching lady said as she stooped down and picked up a moon shell.

"Sure is," I replied.

"My batteries are weak," she complained. "As much as I hate to, I'm heading home before they die."

I understood. Even with a good light I could see only a few steps in front of me. I yearned for a beacon to brighten the beach.

We were three shell seekers on a predawn hunt. If we had waited for the morning light, we would have missed our window of opportunity. The water level would have risen, hiding many of the shells, and there would have been more people to divide the spoil.

This shelling excursion reminds me of our search for the gifts in adversity. Whether we have little or no light, we need to "go out" and retrieve those treasures that can't be gleaned at any other time.

Our natural tendency is to say, "I'll wait a little longer before I start looking; I need more light." We prefer to avoid the scary task of searching in shadowy surroundings. But, no matter how discomforting, we need to seize the opportunities to gather what can't be found at any other time.

After an unwanted divorce, John said, "In the midst of my darkness I learned who God is, that he can be trusted. Christianity is more than something to believe; it's someone to know, and I came to understand him more. Before my divorce, I tended to focus on what I did for God."

Rosene learned more about God, too. For two years, her daughter Cheryl had been in and out of psychiatric hospitals and drug rehabilitation programs. Just when Rosene thought the situation was improving, Cheryl failed to come home for several days. Rosene called the police and reported her missing.

"I imagined her overdosed somewhere. I couldn't shake my fear or that recurring picture in my mind. After talking with the police, God gave me this verse, 'We do not know what to do, but our eyes are upon you' (2 Chronicles 20:12d, NIV).

"My perspective has to be that Cheryl is God's child," Rosene added. "His arms are longer and his reach is greater than mine. Sometimes I believe God wants us to be helpless and walk in darkness, so we can witness his power."

Sallie, whom we met in chapter six, also discovered something in the midst of her troubles. While struggling with the hurt and anger over her son's death, she felt God say, "Death is nothing to me; I'm more powerful than death. I'm greater than all these things."

"At that instant," Sallie said, "I was filled with a profound sense of his might and power. It gave me such peace and hope knowing that he can and will take my tragedy and use it."

John, Rosene, and Sallie were able to glean some valuable truths because they confronted the dark times and looked for the gifts in them. In the same way, the three of us on the beach that morning, with varying degrees of light, found more than those who stayed tucked in bed.

Although it's easy to focus on darkness, we need to be mindful of God and the light of his promises. He says, "I will give you the treasures of darkness, riches stored in secret places, so that you may know that I am the Lord, the God of Israel, who summons you by name" (Isaiah 45:3, NIV).

Chapter Fifteen

As It Turned Out

Is that Naomi?" the women in Bethlehem's marketplace inquired of one another.

Overhearing them, Naomi, whose name means pleasant, grumbled, "Why would you call me Naomi? It would be closer to the truth if you call me Mara, for my life has become very bitter. I left here with my husband and two sons, but now I have nothing. The Almighty has taken them away" (adapted from Ruth 1).

Naomi was a destitute woman. With little resources, her future looked bleak at best. Having faced famine and death, she was now filled with despair. Naomi and her foreign daughter-in-law Ruth, hearing that the famine was over, returned home to Bethlehem after years of living in another country.

Because the two women arrived during the barley harvest with little to eat, Ruth suggested, "Why don't I gather the stalks of grain the harvesters have left in the fields?"

"Go see what you can find," Naomi answered.

As it turned out, Ruth chose a field belonging to Boaz, a kind and gentle man who also happened to be a close relative of Naomi's husband.

That evening, Naomi's eyes widened and her hopes soared when she discovered whose field Ruth had chosen and the abundance of grain she had gleaned. Naomi could hardly contain her excitement.

"Boaz is one of our kinsman redeemers," she explained. "He has already shown you compassion today; look how much grain you've gathered. If he is willing, as a close relative, he can deliver us from our plight."

And Boaz did.

At the end of the Book of Ruth we read that after the marriage of Boaz and Ruth, Naomi was given a future and a grandson.

In four short chapters, we read how Naomi's distressed, hopeless life was transformed to one filled with joy, hope, and security.

The Book of Ruth is a tale of God's blessings and restoration, his ability to turn around the most hopeless of situations. It is also a story of divine providence, how God works behind the scenes for our good.

Like Naomi, we usually don't notice God's invisible hand in the midst of our problems until we look back. But God *is* always at work in our circumstances, no matter how difficult or frustrating they may be.

I was reminded of his divine touch one Mother's Day several years ago. It was one of those days when nothing seemed to go right. First, I was disappointed that Kyle did not acknowledge the day. There was no gift, card, or even a "Happy Mother's Day" greeting. I knew it was silly to make such a big deal over this, but I couldn't seem to shake my sadness.

Next, a planned picnic with my mom and aunt turned into a cramped lunch in the car because of blustery cold weather. Convinced that everyone else was having a lovely Mother's Day dinner at a warm, elegant restaurant, my sullen mood deepened.

"Let's go to the conservatory," Aunt Cecelia said, attempting to salvage the afternoon. "There was an article in the paper about a special exhibit of exotic flowers."

The thought of color, beauty, and warmth perked me up, and we were quickly on our way.

Nearing the glass house, we noticed two men digging tulips from the beds around it. Since the flowers were still quite lovely, their removal seemed strange to me.

"Why are you taking out the tulips?" I asked.

"They want to plant the summer annuals in these areas," one man replied.

"What will they do with the bulbs?"

"Sell them," he commented as he continued to dig.

"How much are they?" I questioned.

"Two dollars a bushel." He never looked up.

"Two dollars a bushel! May I buy some?"

"I don't know why not," he answered nonchalantly.

My mind was reeling with excitement. I was already computing how many bushels I could fit in my small trunk.

Minutes later, as I tucked the third and last basket of the bargain bulbs in my car, I felt God whisper, "Happy Mother's Day! I picked something I knew you would enjoy."

Feeling very special, I shut the lid of the trunk. Once again, when I least expected it, God reminded me of his divine touch. He's always at work; I just never know how it will all turn out.

Chapter Sixteen

Creating Distance

Mommy, look! I made the sailboat disappear."

Six-year-old Kyle and I were standing at the top of a tall building as Kyle pressed the tip of his little finger against the glass, causing the sailboat below to vanish from his view.

Although I've often wished I could make my problems disappear under the tip of my finger, I've found creating some distance from them to be the next best thing.

When we're attempting to find the gifts in our troubles, sometimes we get too close to our concerns and lose our perspective. Like looking down from the height of that building, we'll find we are less likely to drown in the details of our struggles when we expand our view. Here are a few suggestions for accomplishing this.

Focus on God and his creation.
In Colossians 3, Paul instructs us to set our minds on things above.

Carol, who had a bone marrow transplant several years after I did, said, "I started to look at the 'big picture' of my life instead of the day-to-day despairs. I focused on God's will for me—his direction and his vision—instead of losing myself in 'doing.'"

In Psalm 121 we read, "I lift up my eyes to the hills—where does my help come from? My help comes from the Lord, the Maker of heaven and earth" (Psalm 121:1-2, NIV).

My journal entry on August 16, 1992:

I so desperately need to get out of my world and into God's. Today as I walked along a dirt path with a lake to my right, pine trees and mountains on my left, and a deep blue sky above, I started to feel the toxic stress drain from my pores.

The frustration and trivialities of life clog my soul and will destroy it if I'm not careful. But as I immerse myself in God and his creation, I begin to inhale a glorious beauty and am reminded of his awesome strength, wisdom, and power.

Get away physically, mentally, and emotionally.

Sam, from West Virginia, watched the health of his wife slowly deteriorate. Because his opportunities to get away were limited, his world became smaller and smaller.

"When I went to the fitness center and lifted weights for an hour, the fog cleared, enabling me to see beyond my current problems," Sam said. "It was enough to keep me going."

Judy, whom I met in Washington, had relocated to the Northwest, only to lose her job after one year. "Ever since I moved from the South I wanted to see the orca whales everyone talked about. But, of course, I concentrated on my career and never made the trip. "When my position was terminated," Judy said, "I worked hard trying to turn a negative situation into a positive one. However, with no job in sight, I became frustrated, discouraged, and just plain stuck.

"Then, one afternoon a group of friends took me on a whale-watching excursion. For two-and-a-half hours those majestic creatures mesmerized us. Their grace and beauty lifted my spirits and somehow put my plight in perspective. I kept thinking, 'Why am I making such a big deal out of this problem? We are just a dot on this earth—so small compared to these whales!' My only regret was that I hadn't taken the time to get away sooner. I felt so renewed!"

My friend Marita Littauer discovered a quick trip to her backyard was all she needed to create some distance.

Over twenty years ago her husband, Chuck, built a large radio-controlled model airplane. This plane, with a five-foot wing span, has traveled with them to eight different houses over the years. In their current home it hangs from the peak of the cathedral ceiling in the family room.

Recently Chuck took the plane to a model airplane show. He spent hours cleaning off the accumulated dust that had firmly attached itself to every surface.

The plane was a hit at the show, and Chuck discovered how valuable it is. Before he returned the plane to its hook on the ceiling, he decided to protect it with plastic dry cleaning bags, advertising and all. Marita, who likes to have a lovely home, felt covering the plane with printed dry cleaning bags went too far. "I'll never be able to entertain again," she wailed.

Realizing her outburst was an overreaction, she went outside and trimmed her roses. As she took a deep breath, the words "love extravagantly" came to mind. Only a week earlier she had decided her personal mission was to love her husband with extravagance.

"Does it really matter if the airplane has bags over it?" she asked herself. "What is more important, that my husband be happy or that I have a lovely home?"

She headed back inside to apologize. However, while Marita

was outside, Chuck had also gotten some distance on the issue. He had decided that she was right, that the bags were really ugly. He took the plane down, removed the dry cleaning bags, and was in the process of replacing them with clear plastic wrap that clings tightly to every curve and doesn't show.

Reach out to others.

"It never fails," said Theresa, who is a single mother of two. "When I get caught up in my problems, reaching out to others who are facing trouble gives me a new perspective. The more difficult my life gets, the more important it becomes that I call or visit someone in need. We both end up feeling encouraged."

Whether we visit someone in the hospital or nursing home, send a note of encouragement, transport an elderly neighbor, or provide assistance to a young mother, we become thankful for what we have, realizing we would not want to trade places.

When the issues in front of us loom larger and larger, it's time to create some distance and catch a glimpse of God's plan. By widening our view, our challenges often temporarily shrink in size or disappear, like the sailboat underneath Kyle's little finger.

Chapter Seventeen

Search, Search, and Search Some More

I refuse to give up!" I declared out loud. "There's just *got* to be another way."

For six years, I had struggled to find a combination of chemical sprays that would prevent insects and disease from disfiguring my hybrid tea roses. But at the end of each growing season, I'd examine the skeletal remains of my roses and say, "They survived, but that's about it."

Part of the problem was my attitude. I had decided that roses were for experienced gardeners and that someday, years from now, I would plant a few in my garden. However, like my unwanted gift of morning glory seeds, I received three rose bushes my first year of gardening.

"I bought these for your garden," my friend had stated proudly as he unloaded the three plastic containers.

"Ohhhh," I moaned, unable to hide my concern. "I don't know if I'm ready for roses yet."

"Sure you are," he quickly replied, like someone who knows *he* doesn't have to worry about taking care of them. "I'll help you plant them."

And so began my relationship with roses. After talking with a few experienced rose growers, I visited a local nursery and brought home rose food, sprays, and the necessary equipment.

Taking care of the roses was lots of work, and I quickly grew tired of it. The truth is, that first year, part of me hoped they would die. It seemed like the easiest solution to my newest responsibility.

But in spite of my pessimistic attitude, the roses endured, and I grew to love them. However, I never managed to find the right combination of sprays to tackle all my problems (rose rust, Japanese beetles, black spot, powdery mildew, and aphids). Over the years, I tried different equipment and various mixtures but with little success.

Then last spring I found a company that deals exclusively with roses and guarantees their combination of sprays. I not only decided to follow their spray program but I also planted more roses. Now I have only one regret: why didn't I discover this formula sooner?

For the first time in seven years my roses had unblemished attractive green foliage all season long, or at least most of the leaves looked great.[10]

Just as I had difficulty finding a solution for my rose problems, we often struggle to gain wisdom in the midst of our troubles. Persistence is necessary as we investigate and observe. We can't give up when success isn't right around the corner.

Eventually, if we do persevere, we'll find value in our unwanted situation. Scripture guarantees it: "If you call out for insight and cry aloud for understanding, and if you look for it as for silver and search for it as for hidden treasure, then you will understand the fear of the Lord and find the knowledge of God. For the Lord gives wisdom, and from his mouth come knowledge and understanding" (Proverbs 2:3-6, NIV).

Take note, though, that there isn't any mention of *when* we'll gain wisdom and understanding. Sometimes we have to search, search, and search some more.

This certainly was true for Jerry Jonas, whose two teenage sons were killed in a car crash. She was devastated and couldn't find any value in her tragedy. "I begged God to give me cancer and let me die," she said. "But I heard one son's voice in my head saying, 'You can't go yet; you have work to do.' That's when I chose to live, no matter how painful it was."

Shortly after that Jerry began Footprints Ministry, which offers support and hope to bereaved parents and their families.

Winifred, who lives in Illinois, was a young mother of an infant and a toddler when her husband was killed in an accident. "As hard as it was," she said, "I knew God was teaching me things I could never learn any other way. I waited and watched so I could learn what I was supposed to out of this incredibly difficult experience."

Debbie, whom we met in chapter five, also became a single parent after her husband's death. "I started looking for God's perspective," she said. "He has another plan for me, so I will surrender and wait until it is revealed. It's scary, but I pray he'll use me."

Pondering the value of our troubles can be like walking through a field of snow during a whiteout. With no houses or markers for reference, we have no idea how much farther we need to go. We could be a quarter of the way, halfway, or very close to our destination. There is no way of telling. But if we're headed in the right direction, our only choice is to keep on going.

In the same way we need to persist until we gain God's perspective. We may become discouraged or frustrated. We may create excuses. We may even wish we were dead. But we must refuse to give up.

Reflection From the Garden

We've discussed viewing our circumstances or the things around us from a new perspective. Have you ever considered drying peonies? I must admit I hadn't until someone suggested it to me.

For years I have dried roses, strawflowers, yarrow, statice, honesty, and baby's breath. Now every season I add my peonies and manage to snatch a few from my mother's garden as well. They have become one of my favorite dried flowers.

Yet, when I mention this idea, the usual response is, "I didn't know peonies could be dried." For some reason, they are *not* included on the lists of everlasting flowers.

If you would like to try this, I recommend cutting your peonies first thing in the morning, after the dew evaporates. Be sure they are fresh, as flowers that have begun to fade lack the vibrancy of those cut right before they peak.

Remove all but a few of the leaves on the stem, tie several flowers together with string, and suspend upside down to dry. I hang mine from a nail in my attic, being certain that the bunches are not too large and each one hangs separately. Depending on the temperature and humidity of the drying area, it can take about one to three weeks for the flowers to dry.

Peonies can be mixed with any other dried flower and arranged in baskets, crocks, or whatever container you prefer.

One of my favorite bouquets is white and pink peonies with baby's breath in a small cut-glass vase.

Part Three

Find the Value

Launch out into the deep and
let down your nets for a catch.

LUKE 5:4, NKJV

Chapter Eighteen

Flowers of the Field

I stepped into the empty elevator, pushed the third floor button, and watched the door begin to close.

"Going up?" a man hollered.

The door jerked, reversing itself, and in walked the very person I was on my way to see—my doctor.

As the door closed again, the silence made me feel uncomfortable. I decided to strike up a conversation.

"I like that hat!"

The words no sooner left my mouth than I desperately wanted to grab them back. Something about his appearance didn't add up, and I suddenly realized the hat was the problem. His ski jacket matched the January weather, but he was wearing a straw hat, the type fit for a beach resort.

With obvious discomfort he glanced down at his feet, looked up at me, and said, "I had a melanoma removed from the top of my head. This hat does the best job of covering the skin graft."

"Ohhhhhhh," I grimaced. "I'm so sorry."

"Yeah, it was a real shocker," he said. "But then you know the feeling."

"Unfortunately, I do."

"You know," he said, "suddenly I find myself looking at life with a whole new intensity."

The elevator stopped, the door opened, and he dashed off to his afternoon appointments, saying, "See you in a few minutes."

Slowly I walked down the hall toward his office reflecting on our conversation. I had entered the elevator focused on my appointments and errands. I exited immersed in a deep truth, one etched in my heart by my own experience.

It was a knowledge that life doesn't go on forever. And sometimes we need to be reminded that it may end sooner than we think.

The doctor and I aren't the only ones who had to face death in order to understand the value of life. Many of those who have come to grips with their mortality have either confronted the possible end of their own life or of someone they love. In either case, it frequently takes a crisis for us to realize we have taken life for granted.

Understanding the fragility of life was the first gift I unwrapped and one I don't ever want to lose.

But if we're not careful, this truth can slowly wander away, like a child on a crowded beach. Just as a throng of people can distract and block the view of the child, the common urgencies of daily life, like paying bills, getting kids off to school, making meals, attending after-school activities, doing laundry, and cleaning house, can cause us to lose sight of the gift of today.

Scripture reminds us that our time on earth is brief. The psalmist says, "Every man at his best state is but vapor" (Psalm 39:5, NKJV) and, "His days are like a passing shadow" (Psalm 144:4, NKJV). Isaiah warns, "All men are like grass, and all their glory is like the flowers of the field" (Isaiah 40:6, NIV).

We are compared to fleeting things like passing shadows,

delicate grass, and dainty flowers rather than the sun, moon, or stars. Yet how many of us compare our lives to that of a perishable rose?

I often walk the country roads near my house, occasionally picking a handful of wild flowers that grace the edge of a field. By the time I get home, the flowers have begun to wilt. Even after being revived in water, they last only a day or two. It's sobering to consider that our radiance is just as short-lived as those tender flowers.

When Julia, a friend from California, returned home from the funeral of her mother, she looked into her husband's eyes and said, "I don't ever want to lose the sense of this. It is only an illusion if we think life is anything but fleeting."

How, like Julia, can we hold on to the sense that life is precious? Although my father was only forty-nine when he died and I have confronted death three times, I still find myself losing the wonder of life. As the child is distracted by the crowded beach, I am distracted by the tasks of daily living.

Rather than waiting for the reality of death to inspire us to live, we can allow the simple things of life, like flowers of the field, to remind us that life is fragile. We must enjoy the wildflowers today, and we must live, *really* live, now.

Yesterday is the Past,
Tomorrow is the Future,
Today is a Gift,
That's why we call it the Present.[11]

Chapter Nineteen

When We Are Weak

I hated being helpless. I denied it. I fought it. Rarely did I accept it. Although I still don't find it comfortable, I learned God can be trusted to provide.

The only way to really experience this truth is to be in a helpless predicament, such as being in the desert without food. When dinner suddenly arrives in a situation like that, you know you had *nothing* to do with it.

That's what life was like for me during my illness, my divorce, and the loss of my job. There was little I could do; yet day after day, week after week, my needs were met.

Of the three situations, the bone marrow transplant was the most terrifying. However, it also taught me the most about trusting God to attend to *every* detail. The transplant was performed in Boston, eight hours and hundreds of miles from my home. My family couldn't make arrangements for my trip home until my blood counts reached an acceptable level. It was imperative that I travel by airplane because a long car ride would be too exhausting. Therefore, when I was given the green light, someone from home would have to fly to Boston, at an astronomical last-minute price, and assist me back to Pennsylvania.

Now, would you believe that a dear friend of mine was in the Boston area visiting her family and stopped in to see me the day the doctor said, "You can begin making plans to go home"?

"I'm heading home Friday evening," Patty said. "You can go with me."

A few days later, as Patty pushed my wheelchair to the taxi curb, I noticed people turning their heads in curiosity. A few actually stopped and stared. I caught my reflection in the hospital window, and what I saw frightened me. A gaunt figure slumped in a wheelchair with a mask over her mouth and nose to guard against infection and a scarf wrapped around her head to hide the baldness.

No sooner had we gotten into the cab than I began to feel nauseated. I tried to open the window and discovered to my dismay that taxi windows only go down about five inches. Luckily, the vehicle stopped for a red light and I opened my door and emptied my stomach in the street.

The car next to us was loaded with teenagers, who assumed I was drunk. They proceeded to mimic my heaving sounds, only *much louder.*

"Knock it off!" Patty yelled. "She just had a bone marrow transplant!"

Instantly, she became my heroine. I would have loved to do what she had done, but I didn't have the strength.

"Put your head on my lap, Georgia."

"I'm so sorry you have to deal with me," I said as I collapsed in humiliation. This was only the first few miles of our trip. *Lord, how am I going to make it home?*

Patty stroked my head as if to say, "Don't worry; we'll get through this together."

Frankly, I knew I wouldn't have invited someone who had just vomited to put her head on my lap. I appreciated Patty's gentle spirit, care, and sensitivity. I knew that *somehow* we would make it and that God had provided me with the perfect travel companion.

But I've also learned it's not just during critical times that we can count on God. He also can be depended on for insignificant things. Take the case of the mouse in our house.

One fall, when no one was looking, several mice scampered into our garage, sneaked into the recreation room, and set up housekeeping. I managed to catch all of them in mousetraps—except one.

"We have a smart mouse at our house," Kyle told his friends. That mouse could lick the peanut butter off a trap and not set it off. Finally one morning I cornered the critter in the downstairs bathroom, only to have him slip under the door and escape.

It wasn't until I gave up that God showed me what he could do. I remember it well. I had checked the mousetrap that morning. The tiny morsel of cheese was gone, but there was no mouse in the trap.

"That's it!" I said heading out the door for a weekend trip. "I give up."

Days later I arrived back home and dashed straight to the downstairs bathroom. An oblong object with a tail was floating in the commode. I peered closer.

It was *the* mouse—waterlogged.

I sometimes wonder if God purposefully waits until we are certain we can't do something before he rescues us. Paul said it best: "For when I am weak, then I am strong" (2 Corinthians 12:10, NIV). It is in our utter powerlessness that we experience and can best see God's awesome capabilities.

Adversity also gives those close to us a chance to observe God's provisions. Irene, who attends my writers' group, discovered this when her husband Robert had five major operations in ten years. Then, just when she thought their life might be returning to normal, they were told he had a serious form of leukemia with little hope for recovery.

"Through all the difficulties," Irene said, "the Lord was there and true to his word; 'For I am the Lord, your God, who takes hold of your right hand and says to you, Do not fear; I will help you'" (Isaiah 41:13, NIV).

Irene's cousin voiced this same thought in a letter when she wrote, "We see how the Lord upholds you [Irene], so in the same way, we know when we face difficult circumstances, he will be there for us as well."

When my friend Candy was three years old her father died in a car accident. Today, Candy has a speaking ministry and often talks about "No accidents with Christ." Candy likes to tell about a T-shirt she received for her fiftieth birthday. On it was written, "I'm not 50, I'm 18 with 32 years of experience!"

"One woman I know said she wouldn't want to go back to being eighteen again," Candy relates, "unless she could go back knowing what she knows now.

"I feel the same way," Candy says. "I wouldn't want to go back to being eighteen again 'for all the tea in China,' unless I could go back knowing what I know now. And *if I could* go back knowing what I know now, if I could change *anything*, it would be that I would trust God more. I would trust God more in every area of my life!"

I agree. And I'd cry out to him sooner, much sooner. Then I would wait ... and watch him work.

Chapter Twenty

I Want My Flowers While I'm Living

"Do you love to garden?" I asked my visitor as I sat on my back steps and watched her dig a portion of my hosta. The warm spring sun felt wonderful after the long winter. "I mean, is it something that causes you to lose track of time?"

"Oh, absolutely!" She pressed her foot down on top of the shovel, then stopped and looked up. "My mother used to say, 'I want my flowers while I'm living, not when I'm dead.'"

Placing her one hand on her hip for emphasis, she added, "And I feel the same way."

"Wow!" I gasped. "That says it all, doesn't it? I want *my* flowers while I'm living, too."

Unlike my friend, however, I didn't learn that from my family. Flowers were considered a luxury when I was growing up. The only ones we had around our house had been planted by previous owners. Somehow they had managed to survive in spite of their neglect.

When I was in fourth grade, my family moved to the country. My parents planted an extensive vegetable garden, but no flowers. I grew up believing flowers were only for the wealthy.

Illness taught me that flowers have much to give, and they soon became my passion. I realized I didn't have to be rich to enjoy their beauty.

It was a gradual process, aided by incidents like a dear friend's placing a bouquet of yellow daffodils on my chemotherapy chair or baskets and vases of brilliant flowers brightening my hospital room.

Later, during my slow recovery, I found that by sitting in my flower garden I was able to focus on God and his creation rather than my pain.

But it wasn't until I became strong enough to get my hands in the dirt that my love for flowers really "blossomed." That's when I knew I wanted flowers to decorate my life, not only my grave.

Passion is another gift often found in the midst of devastating losses. We discover who we really are, what we love, and what gives us a sense of meaning.

My newfound passion added so much joy, purpose, and meaning to my life that I wanted to pass this concept on to Kyle. But I wasn't sure how to do so. Unfortunately in my teenage son's vocabulary, passion often referred to strong feelings attached to things that were not necessarily in his best interest.

One summer afternoon after a swim meet, we threw his gear in the trunk of the car and began the long drive home.

"Mom," Kyle said, "I'm just not sure what it is I want to do with my life after graduation."

"Well, what do you like best?" I asked.

"Lots of things."

"Can you list some of them?"

"Well, I like sports ... but I really want to be able to make lots of money."

I felt myself tensing up. Money shouldn't be the major issue, but how could I change his focus? I prayed a quick prayer.

"Kyle, if we were rich, really wealthy—I mean, we had so much money that you would never have to work the rest of your life—what would you do?"

"Oh, that's easy!" he quickly replied. "I'd coach swimming and write."

His response caught me off guard. I had expected his answer to be more along the lines of sailing around the world with a lovely woman.

"Well, there's your answer. If coaching and writing are the desires of your heart, go for it."

Kyle smiled.

It was one of those rare moments when we really connected on the same channel with no emotional static. I breathed a contented sigh, realizing that he understood more about passion than I thought.

Doing what you enjoy sounds simple, yet we manage to make it complex. However, when we follow the passions of our hearts, we will discover true joy and real wealth.

Chapter Twenty-One

Savor the Moment

Kyle leaped up the steps of the school bus.

"Go get 'em, tiger!" I said, clicking the camera.

I had taken Kyle's picture on the first day of school ever since kindergarten. It was a tradition. Now that he was in seventh grade, I was amazed he was still willing to cooperate. Perhaps it was because he was the first child on the bus, and none of his friends were watching.

Kyle found a seat in the back of the bus, flashed a big smile, and waved as the bus headed down our winding country road.

Surprised, but pleased, I quickly raised my arm, waving the biggest good-bye I could muster as the yellow bus disappeared. I continued to stand there for awhile. Never again would it be Kyle's first day in seventh grade, and I wanted to savor this time and carefully tuck away the memory.

I'm not certain when it happened, but at some point I learned to accept the uncertainty of life by cherishing each moment. It is all we have and all we need. But we don't always understand this until adversity teaches us that in spite of all our best-laid plans, we can't determine the future. Then almost as a last resort—a way of consoling ourselves—we tune in to the present moment and accidentally stumble over a gift—the here and now.

We tend to perceive seconds as being trivial, perhaps because they are so brief and pass so quickly. We often dwell on past events or become consumed with the future. However, according to God's Word, "We are born in a moment, we die in a moment, and at Christ's return we will be transformed in a moment" (paraphrase of 1 Corinthians 15:51).

Children are naturals at focusing on the present. A walk with my five-year-old niece confirmed this. In just a few minutes, she stopped to gaze at a bee drawing nectar from a flower, pointed out an ant crossing our path with a morsel of food, and shouted with delight as a monarch butterfly fluttered a few feet in front of us.

Most of us outgrow this approach to life, as we do our pink smocked dresses. Fortunately, sixty-year-old Rosie, whom I met at a garden retreat, did not. When Rosie arrived home after being hospitalized with a serious heart attack, she sniffed the grass.

"I know it sounds silly," she smiled, "but the smell of grass has always been special to me. While I was in the hospital, there were many days I didn't know if I would ever get to relish that smell again. I'm grateful that I did."

Delicate details fill and enrich the present. Sights, sounds, feelings, tastes, and smells all make today special. When Rosene's daughter repeatedly tried to commit suicide, Rosene, introduced in chapter fourteen, concentrated on small things to take her mind off the chaos.

"I'd focus on the tiniest flower in my garden that had made it through the cold earth," she said. "I'd take it inside the house and marvel at its markings. One morning, I obtained such delight at the way each branch on a tree outside my window was completely encased in ice after a winter storm.

"I was very depressed the day I noticed that the pussy willows had opened," Rosene continued. "So I cut a sprig and put it on the dash of my car. As I drove to the hospital to visit my daughter I looked at the fuzzy gray nodes and remembered that here was a sign of spring and new life."

In "Exhaust the Little Moment," Anna Quindlen suggests, "Embrace the little things of life that sometimes get left in the dust of our frenetic schedules. Without the inner satisfaction that comes with them, our accomplishments will be nothing more than the stuff of résumés. And a résumé is cold comfort on a winter night."[12]

Simple things like running through a snowdrift, dancing in the rain, shuffling through fallen leaves, opening the sunroof on a balmy winter day, or savoring a sunset nourish our souls.

When Kyle was small, we had "Time Alone," a time each day when I would stop whatever I was doing and play with him. It helped to cut down on the number of times I'd have to say, "When Mommy finishes the laundry, we'll go outside and play." or, "When Mommy finishes the dinner dishes, I'll help you with that game."

Although our "time alone" was invaluable, it didn't surpass the unexpected events that cropped up each day, like the turtle inching across our driveway or the three deer nibbling in the field outside our picture window.

Life doesn't begin when the children graduate, when we retire, when we get that new job or degree or home. It begins now, and this is the minute to treasure. Erma Bombeck captured this idea in one of her last editorials before she died.

If I Had My Life to Live Over:

... I would have invited friends over to dinner even if the carpet was stained and the sofa faded.

I would have eaten the popcorn in the "good" living room and worried much less about the dirt when someone wanted to light a fire in the fireplace....

I would have sat on the lawn with my children and not worried about grass stains....

Instead of wishing away nine months of pregnancy, I'd have cherished every moment and realized that the wonderment growing inside me was the only chance in life to assist God in a miracle.

When my kids kissed me impetuously, I would never have said, "Later. Now go get washed up for dinner."

There would have been more "I love yous"... more "I'm sorrys" ... but mostly, given another shot at life, I would seize every minute, look at it and really see it ... live it ... and never give it back.[13]

Like Erma Bombeck, I have missed the opportunities of the moment far more than I like to admit. But I'm learning.

Recently, while speaking at a conference, I dashed back to my room to grab the notes for my next seminar.

As I turned to leave, something outside the window caught my eye. I looked again and saw an elegant blue heron along the water's edge.

Slowly I moved closer to the window and watched. I had been to this conference center many times before but had never seen a blue heron.

Jutting its long slender neck forward, the bird took one graceful step and stopped. After a few moments it brought the other leg forward next to the first and paused again. It reminded me of a bride walking down the aisle.

I could feel my frantic spirit settle. The heron's deliberately slow movement was in direct contrast to the fast-paced whirl of the conference.

"Georgia," God whispered, "slow down or you'll miss the beauty around you."

I continued to gaze at the stately bird until it disappeared. Then I sauntered back to the conference feeling refreshed. Once again God had adjusted my priorities, reminding me to slow down, to savor the moment, and to find his joy.

Chapter Twenty-Two

Comfort in Pain

The telephone rang next to my bed. I managed to roll halfway, and with a trembling hand I struggled to reach the receiver.

Another ring.

Thrusting my hand toward the phone, I gave it all I had.

Success! "Hull - lo."

My heart leaped as I heard, "Hi, Mom! Did you get rid of your fever?"

"No."

"What's your temperature?"

"Still 104."

Silence.

Even at age ten, Kyle knew the seriousness of a prolonged fever during a bone marrow transplant. I wanted to blurt out how horrible I felt. I wanted to tell him about the piercing pain and the emptiness of not being able to hug him. I wanted to tell him that I might never be home again. I wanted to ask the question that had haunted me for days, "Kyle, do you know how much your mother loves you?" Instead, I asked, "How was school today?"

"Didn't go to school today; it's Saturday."

"I'm sorry ... it's hard to keep track of time.... I sleep most of the day."

"Had my soccer game today."

"Sure wish I could have been there. Was it fun?"

"It was OK. Well, got to go. I love you."

"I love you."

The tears welled up in my eyes as I hung up the phone. My throat felt like I had swallowed the world.

"Please, God, please let me get well so I can go home to Kyle."

It had been three weeks since I kissed him good-bye and headed to Dana Farber Cancer Institute in Boston. Missing him hurt more than my physical suffering.

I wondered if the ravaging fever would *ever* end. How much weaker could I get? How much longer could I hang on?

The door of my isolated room opened. My nurse walked in wearing a surgical jacket, rubber gloves and a mask. She reached for my right arm.

"Time for some blood samples," she said. "Please make a fist."

I began to pray. The last time it had taken four sticks of the needle to get blood for the laboratory samples. Taking blood was just one more torture technique of modern medicine.

As I tightened my fist, she searched for a "good" vein. Given all the chemotherapy I had endured, this was a real challenge.

"Let's try this one."

She probed hard with the needle in the center of one vein to break the scar tissue. It burned and stung for a second, then relief.

"I hate blood tests. Just hate them."

My eyes focused on the pale blue sky outside my window. A

few minutes later she announced, "Finished ... anything I can do for you before I leave?"

"Yes, I want to be warm and healthy."

She glanced at me with an I-know-you-are-hurting-but-you-know-we-are-trying-to-help-you look.

"Let's hope this fever breaks; you'll feel much better when it does. It's been almost a week now."

How well I knew.

The next morning, however, I was weaker and colder; a biting chill pervaded every ounce of my being. How I yearned for relief.

A greeting card hanging on the bulletin board in front of my bed caught my eye. The poem "Footprints in the Sand" was tacked next to a picture of Kyle. I prayed and silently wept. *Please, Lord, help me. I want to live and be a mother to my son.*

An image appeared in my mind, as vivid as the card on the bulletin board. It was an image of Jesus walking in the sand along the ocean's edge, carefully carrying my weak, limp, fevered body in his powerful arms. I sobbed.

"Lord, put me down," I murmured. "Surely there are others more ill or more important than I."

Stronger words seemed to be assuring me, "No, you need me. I am here for you. You are special, too."

A beautiful feeling of love and peace filled me. I wasn't alone. The loss of my physical strength seemed to be replaced by a different kind of strength, a spiritual one. The serenity I felt was accompanied by knowing that if I did live, my life would never be the same.

Although I don't ever want to return to that feeble condition, there are times when I long for the spiritual closeness and peace I sensed that day.

Suffering draws us close to God; we experience his comfort

and get a taste of heaven. The paradox is that we believe tranquillity comes from creature comforts, earthly luxuries—the very things that can separate us from our Lord and give us a taste of hell.

In an informal survey, I asked women who had encountered troubling times to list the most precious gifts or blessings that came from adversity. Regardless of the nature of their difficulties, the common response was that they had experienced the love, security, and comfort of God during dark times.

"There's nothing *on earth* that can soothe my pain," Sallie, introduced in chapter six, said, referring to the agony of losing her twenty-year-old son in an automobile accident.

"Only the Lord and his Spirit eased my suffering and gave me comfort. God's grace kept me from sinking. It was there *with* the pain. Grace didn't remove the torment—grace came along beside it. I've learned through this tragedy that God's grace is sufficient."

I met Laura Beth at a retreat in Maryland. She told me that when she was five-and-a-half-months pregnant her doctors discovered she had lost almost all her amniotic fluid. She was put on restricted bed rest, had to lie on her right side, and could get up only when absolutely necessary. Unfortunately, at seven months she went into labor and delivered a stillborn baby girl.

"Since then, I have had two healthy sons, but I will always grieve the loss of my tiny daughter," Laura Beth said. "However, it gave me the chance to experience firsthand the 'peace that surpasses all understanding' and witness its amazing impact on those around me."

My friend Betsy was profoundly influenced by the beautiful peace her mother carried through extremely difficult times. "My mother had thirteen children but lost ten of them during her life. One of her daughters was killed in a plane crash, another committed suicide, and one as a newborn was dropped by a nurse and lived only for seven years, totally paralyzed.

"Through all that suffering my mother had an inner strength and contentment that was amazing. Although as children we grew up in the church, we never understood the source of my mother's tranquillity. We didn't understand it was her relationship with God that carried her through the tragedies and gave her comfort.

"Years later when my sister and I both went through divorces and endured drug problems with some of our children, we were so devastated we began searching for something to relieve our pain.

"My mother would quietly say, 'I think it would help if you went to church.'

"Unfortunately, it wasn't until I was overwhelmed by the heartache of Mother's death that it finally clicked. She had lived the Christian life but never preached it. Although my mother only had an eighth-grade education, she was a very wise lady and an expert on living with pain.

"If Mother could see my sister, niece, and me today, she would be elated. We not only go to church, but we attend a weekly Bible study. We realize it was her relationship with the Lord that kept her going and gave her a deep sense of peace. We now know we, too, can go through anything."

Paul wrote that our Lord "comforts us *in all* our troubles" (2 Corinthians 1:4, NIV, emphasis mine). Comfort and pain—how can they both occupy our lives at the same time? This is a paradox that only God can fully understand but we can fully experience.

Chapter Twenty-Three

Sharing Our Struggles

When I was first diagnosed with cancer, I didn't want people to know. I had problems accepting the diagnosis, and keeping it from others helped me to pretend it didn't exist. I even labeled the file folder containing my medical bills "Breast Lump," not "Breast Cancer."

"Georgia," one friend said, "you're going to miss out on a lot of love and prayers by keeping this to yourself." But she respected my wishes and never mentioned it again.

Finally, after my recurrence, the walls of denial crumbled, and I learned my friend was right. I did need to share my illness as well as my struggles and be willing to receive the help of others. A year and a half later, when I prepared to go to Boston for the transplant, I informed everyone I knew, asking for their prayers. I discovered their love and support to be invaluable.

Like me, Michelle found it easier to give assistance than to accept it. "I'd often say, 'Oh, I'll be fine,' even if it wasn't true," she stated. "I had to learn how to receive. When I did, I was amazed how excited people were to help. One friend said to me, 'Don't deprive me of the opportunity to give to you.' In a way it was the best six months of my life," she added, speaking of her chemotherapy treatments. "I was surrounded by the most caring friends a person could have."

Carol, whom we met in chapter sixteen, said this about her troubling times: "What a blessing it was to see how devoted my husband is and how much he really loves me."

I met Nancy at a women's retreat, and she told me how important her friends were after her husband's adulterous relationship. "I've gained true friends," she said, "and an appreciation of what their love and support mean to me."

Adversity can pull down artificial barriers, sweep away superficial layers, and allow us to gain an intimate view of our friends and family. Some folks turn bitter and angry when trouble arrives, but it is the well-rooted relationships that will survive regardless of drought, gale force winds, or frigid weather.

I call the caring people who love us "flowers" because they add such beauty and fragrance to our lives. When we are willing to share our struggles, we are often pleasantly surprised to learn:

"Flowers" find ways to lend a hand.

Although they can't solve all of our problems, "flowers" find ways to help. While I was making the arrangements for my long absence during the bone marrow transplant, Kyle was my biggest concern.

"I have to be away from home for at least five weeks, and I'm worried what effect this will have on him," I agonized to my friend Patricia.

In response, Patricia bought me a month's supply of children's greeting cards as well as the stamps to mail them. At her suggestion, I wrote a message inside each card such as, "You are getting lots of kisses through the air, ... Never forget I love you, ... Looking forward to hearing how your day went."

I packed the signed, sealed, stamped, and addressed cards

in my suitcase. Each day while I was hospitalized, a nurse mailed one for me, allowing Kyle to receive a continuous stream of letters. They gave him something to look forward to and provided me with the feeling that I was doing *something* as his mother.

"Flowers" lift our spirits.

The night before Michelle's first chemotherapy treatment, her friend Sharon called.

"Michelle, I was just reading Matthew and something struck me that I hadn't noticed before," she said excitedly. "Remember the story of Jesus walking on the water?"

"Yeah."

"Well, Peter was at his highest spiritual point ever," Sharon said. "He was strong in faith and physically at a high point, he felt elated ... he was actually walking on water with his Lord. But as Peter started walking toward Jesus the wind picked up, he became afraid and started to sink. As soon as he cried out, 'Lord, save me!' Jesus reached out and scooped him up."

"That's a beautiful story," Michelle replied. "I get it, Peter lost his focus on Jesus and became afraid and began to sink."

"Well, that's not really the point," Sharon said.

"OK, I get it now," Michelle said. "The point is that I need to pray to Jesus to lift me up."

"No, that's not the point either," Sharon said. "The point is this: You don't have to do anything. Just let him scoop you up. He will carry you; just let him."

"Flowers" offer specific assistance.

"What surprised me most was how many people took the initiative to do things rather than say, 'Let me know if there is anything I can do,'" Michelle said.

Every week Michelle receives a call from one friend who had breast cancer.

"She knows the anger, the sadness, the issues, and the challenges that I face. She provides me with the opportunity to vent and unload. She can genuinely understand what I am feeling."

Another friend organized the "Michelle chemomobile," which provided different friends to drive Michelle to her twelve treatments.

Her friend said, "We had a theme: chemo can be fun."

"And they really did make it fun," Michelle agreed. "They picked me up at my doorstep, stopped by my favorite coffee shop, and brought new magazines and lists of jokes to enjoy during the chemo treatments."

It's comforting to know that there are still people who are willing to lend a hand, if we allow them.

Recently, after I had spoken at a conference, a man with deep sad eyes said to me, "My wife's cancer has returned, and she won't let me tell anyone. I have to keep the pain and the problems all inside."

My heart ached for them both as I remembered how I had felt. I said to him, "Tell her I've found you miss out on a lot of love and prayers by keeping this to yourself."

Sometimes we need to swallow our pride, admit we are weak, and allow others to assist. Their love makes all the difference when we're suffering; it is a real gift to our souls.

Chapter Twenty-Four

Eliminating
the "Someday…"
and "If Only …"

"I t's about the size of a grapefruit," the doctor said after my ultrasound test. He was referring to an ovarian tumor that had been discovered during my annual exam. Given my history with breast cancer, the doctor did not paint a pretty picture. We scheduled surgery, and I cancelled a speaking engagement in California.

As I drove home that day, my head throbbed. I hadn't seen this coming. The only possible hints were that my jeans fit more snugly and I was experiencing more fatigue.

In spite of the report, though, I felt a peace that came from knowing I had tried my best to focus on the things that mattered most to me. My relationships, especially with Jesus and my son, had grown deeper and richer over the last few years.

I could not have always made that statement. Eight years earlier I had a stack of unfinished business that reached the ceiling. It was a pile of "somedays."

"Someday I want to see the cherry blossoms in Washington,

D.C. Someday I'm going to sit down and write my son a 'Did-I-ever-tell-you' letter. Someday I'll ..."

With the recurrence of breast cancer my "somedays" had turned into "if onlys." "If only I wouldn't have taken my job so seriously. If only I would have spent more time with my family. If only I wouldn't have felt the need to get straight A's in my graduate studies. If only ..."

When I arrived home from the doctor's, I pulled into the garage, propped my arms on the steering wheel, buried my head, and prayed for strength and wisdom.

As was true years earlier, I knew I needed to plan for the worst but continue praying for the best.

Almost immediately, I felt an urgent need to write a letter to Kyle. Rather than a "cold" will I wanted him to have something "warm and caring"—a handwritten note containing a permanent record of my love, faith, and values. It would be something that he could read over and over again, in case I wasn't around to tell him myself.

But first, I had to share the devastating news with him. Since he was still at swim practice, I had some time to gather my courage. My vision blurred with tears thinking of what we had gone through over the last several years. How I dreaded what I had to do.

I had just finished dinner when I heard the garage door open. Immediately, Kyle leaped up the steps to the living room.

"What's going on?" he barked loudly, his eyes filled with concern. "This afternoon a doctor kept calling here every fifteen minutes asking for you. What did he want?"

I sighed, evading eye contact, and motioned for us to sit down. The tears I had been determined to hold back gushed down my cheeks.

"Kyle, I had a routine checkup, and they discovered another

tumor. I'm scheduled for surgery in a few days."

"How serious is it?" Kyle asked, visibly cringing.

"Only God knows the answer to that."

I paused to gather more strength, blew my nose, and whispered, "Kyle, I won't be able to go to your state swim meet."

"But you have to," he pleaded.

"Believe me, I want to, but I'll still be in the hospital."

I blew my nose again. Taking another deep sigh I asked, "Kyle, will you pray with me?"

He jumped to his feet.

"I'm not praying with you," he raged. "You picked the worst time for this to happen. Now I don't even know if I can swim at states, let alone win."

He stomped off to his room and slammed the door.

Stunned, hurt, and alone, I wept. Then I got up, stumbled to my room, and tucked myself into bed. Reaching over to my nightstand, I grabbed my journal and wrote what Kyle wouldn't allow me to say.

March 5,1997

Kyle, I love you. I thank God for you. If I'm not with you much longer, we'll make the time we do have count. Don't give up on your faith. It's OK to be angry with God. But just remember, life without our Lord isn't worth living. But with faith in Jesus, we can touch the lives of others, we can know we will make a difference—no matter how long we live!

That's all I had written when the phone started ringing. Friends, who had heard the news, called to say they were praying for me.

My heart broke again later that evening when I stopped outside Kyle's closed bedroom door to say good night and overheard him talking on the phone.

"My mom can't go to states," he said. "I'm afraid she's dying."

Such life-disrupting events force us to reexamine our lives. They make us stop and think about what is important. They cause us to readjust our priorities.

Although I never got to California that year to speak, I did send two questions to the women in the audience. One was, "If you found out tomorrow that your life was threatened, what would you change?" The other was, "What matters most to you, and are you taking the time to do it?"

That second question haunted me both before and after my surgery, even after I was miraculously handed a new lease on life. "Well, Georgia, I have good news," my doctor said as he stood at the end of my bed. "We were able to completely remove the tumor; you don't need any further treatments."

"Thank you, God!" I sighed with relief.

I still had some unfinished business. It was a dream God had tucked in my heart years earlier, during my recovery from the transplant: *Someday I want to write a book to help others restore their lives after loss, a book that will encourage them to move beyond existing or merely surviving to a brand new life.* It was time to turn that dream into a reality.

Sydney Harris wrote, "Regret for the things we did can be tempered by time; it is regret for the things we did not do that is inconsolable."[14]

I needed to get writing; I didn't want to die with any "if onlys...."

Chapter Twenty-Five

Something Even Better

I hung the odd-shaped gold ornament on my Christmas tree with a chuckle. *What a story it had!* The decoration had been given to me the previous holiday. But it wasn't just any bauble; it was a gift with a history.

For several years, my Bible study group had played a game at our Christmas dinner party that went like this. Each couple brought two wrapped presents: one that they had selected and purchased, the other, an "undesirable" one. Both packages were beautifully wrapped and placed under the hostess' tree.

After dessert and coffee, everyone drew a number. The person with number one picked a package and opened it. Then in numerical order, we chose gifts from the pile and opened them. If we didn't like the contents of the package, we had one chance to force a trade with anyone who possessed an opened gift we preferred. Obviously, those with the highest numbers took home something desirable. There were always a few kind, generous souls who kept their unwanted parcel rather than swipe another's treasure.

Laughter brought us to tears when items such as an old shell lamp or a dusty faded silk flower arrangement were opened. But true to the saying that one man's trash is another's treasure, invariably someone excitedly carted home one of the presents meant to be a joke.

Most of the closet relics, however, ended up in the trash shortly after the party, except for one unwanted gift that showed up year after year. Disguised in different size boxes or bags, this present was guaranteed to bring hoots or giggles. It was a dark brown plaster plaque of a knight, left over from the Mediterranean decorating fad of the '70s. This brown enamel picture was as traditional for us as the Christmas poinsettia. The annual holiday party question became, "Who will get the plaque?"

One year, when Jeff had the distinction of taking it home, he decided to make it into something better. Using a band saw, he cut the plaque into randomly shaped pieces, creating a jigsaw puzzle. And, you guessed it, he tucked it under the Christmas tree at our next holiday party.

Brian received the honors that year. "Oh, no!" he gasped amidst laughter.

Not to be outdone by Jeff, Brian's wife, Amy, secretly spray painted the puzzle pieces gold, glued on glimmering sparkles, and added a ribbon for hanging. The following Christmas she presented each of us with a small tissue-filled gift bag. Inside was our "piece of the plaque"—a tree decoration.

Like the gradual transformation of the unwanted plaque to a puzzle to an ornament, God uses undesirable events to change us. Just ask Sharon Burniston, a young mother with three children. I met Sharon, who also is Michelle's friend in chapter twenty-three, at her church's annual retreat. She is slowly losing her sight to Stargardt's disease, a young person's version of macular degeneration, which causes blindness in the elderly.

Sharon's impaired vision affects every area of her life.

Resigning from her teaching position was only one of many losses.

"One morning I was trying to read a newspaper article and having more trouble than ever before," Sharon said. "I knew I could read it if I would just work a little bit harder. I struggled and struggled with it and finally threw the paper across the room.

"Suddenly I remembered seeing one of my students doing the same thing when he didn't want to finish a difficult assignment. I had spent six years as a teacher glibly telling students to 'work just a little bit harder,' never realizing what that struggle truly felt like. The insight I gained has helped me to understand other people's limitations and frustrations.

"But in spite of my challenges," Sharon continued, "every time I face another loss, when I stop looking inward and feeling sorry for myself and begin to look outward to find a solution, God has always given me something even better than I expected. Losing my sight has allowed me to see the richness of life and to know *absolutely* that God is with me, constantly guiding me and showing me ways to achieve anything I truly need. I don't know where I'll end up, but wherever I go, God will be right there beside me, every step of the way. I can *see that* clearly."

Sharon's contentment, wisdom, and genuine humility are not born out of sufficiency and ease but out of deprivation, frustration, and pain. By relying on God, she has changed into something even better.

Like Sharon, Renea, whom we met in chapter five, at first dwelled on what had been taken from her. "Before my head injury," Renea said, "I had no patience and tolerated very little. I had gone to college to be a teacher, but right before my student teaching, I decided I didn't have the empathy needed to be an elementary school teacher.

"Suddenly, years later, as a result of my trauma, I met people in the hospital and rehabilitation center who were so compassionate. Their help and concern touched me. I began working on being patient, kind, and accepting of others. Now I've found the most wonderful part of me is shining through—the unique individual that the Lord created me to be."

I, too, remember dwelling on what I lost rather than on how I was changing. I especially despised the loss of my stamina and strength. I wanted to be able to glide from one strenuous chore to the next rather than lie down and rest after every task. However, one day when I rode past an elderly neighbor's home, I realized how I had been transformed by my circumstances.

My neighbor stood dejectedly in his front yard, slumped against his rake for support. He had stopped to catch his breath and was staring at the tiny pile of leaves he had just raked. I surveyed the remaining leaves blanketing his one-acre property and also felt overwhelmed by the small dent his efforts had made. How I wanted to stop and encourage him. Here was a man, like me, who had prided himself on his achievements and accomplishments. Now weakened by the accumulating years, he felt his job was impossible.

Knowing he would be embarrassed by my display of concern, I smiled and waved as I passed. Immediately I began to pray, "Lord, give him the strength to finish the task, or bring someone to help him."

My neighbor's image remained with me that day, and I prayed for him several more times. It was an image that in earlier years may not have concerned me. I probably would have zipped past him on my way to work or graduate school, without a second thought. I would not have been sensitive to his frail condition, nor would I have felt it so imperative to pray for his needs.

I like the person I am today more than the person I was before my troubles. However, I didn't like the circumstances that triggered this change. Comfort and convenience would have been my choice, but the tough times proved to be far more beneficial. I may not be the golden ornament on the Christmas tree, but at least I've made it to the puzzle piece stage.

When people face a major upheaval, they often say, "My life is over." Maybe it is. Or maybe it is the beginning of an opportunity to become something even better.

Reflection From the Garden

The best advice, for anyone with a garden, is don't neglect the weeds. The longer they are ignored, the deeper the roots grow and the stronger the plant becomes. I learned this the hard way.

One afternoon, while struggling with an especially weedy area, I contemplated the desirability of a weed. Given the choice, most gardeners would eliminate these plants forever. Is there any value in weeds? I may be "stretching" it, but these are the benefits I found:

- Therapeutic outlet—We can release all our frustrations and resentments on weeds. We can yell at them, mistreat them, or destroy them, without hurting anything of value.

- Physical exercise—Their very existence gets us moving and keeps us active as we attempt to eradicate them.

- Food source—Although I don't like to eat them, my uncle always thought that spring dandelions were a real delicacy.

- Valuable teaching tool—When I'm in my garden, I have the choice of focusing on the weeds or the flowers. If I focus on the weeds, I feel discouraged or defeated. If I focus on the flowers, I feel optimistic. In the same way, I can either focus on the cares of this world or my relationship with Christ. The former leaves me feeling overwhelmed while the latter encourages me.

- Awareness of garden—Often while I'm down on my knees pulling weeds, I discover a cherished plant that needs special attention. If it weren't for the weeds, the problem may have gone unnoticed.

Weeds do keep us busy. But when we attend to their removal, we are tending to our gardens and ourselves.

Part Four

Take the Risk

Be transformed by the
renewing of your mind.

ROMANS 12:2, NIV

Chapter Twenty-Six

Facing Our Fears

I never yearned to be a writer. I never wanted to write a book. But life's experiences have a way of changing you, your dreams, and your desires.

After the dust from my divorce and transplant settled, I had an irresistible urge to write a book about restoring our lives after loss. There was one major problem. I couldn't write, at least in a way that anyone would choose to read.

I have four college degrees, with highest honors in each, but there are two lonely C's on my college transcripts—in English and writing. And I worked hard to get those C's! During my freshman year in college, I spent my Christmas vacation writing a paper to improve my English grade.

After my instructor read what I had written, she called me into her office and threatened to fail me.

"What's wrong?" I asked.

"It's quite obvious to me that someone else wrote this paper for you," she said. "This is so much better than anything *you* ever did."

Somehow I managed to convince her it was my work, but the experience was demoralizing and left me with yet another open wound on my writer's soul. The incident only confirmed what some of my high school teachers and friends had already told me—I couldn't write.

I remember a professor in graduate school saying, "We all think we have a book inside of us." I smirked and thought, *Not me. I'd rather die than write a book.*

Well, I did almost die, and in the process I learned things that could help others. But write a book? *Georgia, are you insane?* However, the thought of passing on what I had learned continued to haunt me.

Finally, one day I jotted some ideas in a journal. And that was the day the dragonlike voices within came to life.

"What do you think you're doing?" they taunted. "You'll never write a book," they jeered. "Who will ever read what you have written?"

Tears filled my eyes as I put down my pen and journal. It was true; whatever gave me the idea I might be able to communicate with words? It took another month to work up the courage to scribble just a few more sentences.

Like a seed concealed in the dark ground, I continued to keep the desire to record my experiences hidden. Eventually, though, the seed germinated until I thought I would explode if I didn't share my book idea with my dearest friends. With their love and encouragement, I began the slow, painstaking project of learning how to write in spite of the voices which kept shouting, "Give up. You'll never succeed."

I wrote lengthy journal entries, went to writers' conferences, and even joined a writing critique group. Although invaluable and something I would recommend, my writers' group was another humbling experience. After hearing the other women present their delightful, well-crafted works, I'd present something I had written, and in a polite, friendly manner they would trash it.

Using their suggestions, I would rewrite it and return one month later only to hear, "Georgia, you must learn to 'show not tell.'" This was a concept I couldn't seem to grasp. Near tears I would repeatedly ask, "But how do I do that?"

Over and over I was told that "show, don't tell" refers to creating a picture with words, like a movie clip—incorporating as many of the senses as possible so the reader can see, feel, hear, smell, or taste whatever it is you're describing.

After those critiques it usually took me a week to write again. "Face it," the dragonlike voice whispered, "those women are just being kind. They think your writing is horrible."

It would have been so easy to give up, but there was always that strong sense of calling to complete the book. When I shared my message with others and saw how people were visibly touched, I knew I had to keep plugging away.

One enthusiastic comment like "Let me know when your book is published; I'll buy one" could inspire me for weeks.

It was six long years before I submitted my first book manuscript to several editors at a writers' conference, fully expecting to see "Would suggest you attend some writing classes as your skills have much to be desired" on their response sheets.

However, not one of the editors said that. In fact one actually said she liked my writing voice. I returned home elated, while most of the conferees left discouraged that no one was interested in their manuscripts.

It was several more years until *the* call finally came from an editor. "I have good news, your proposal has been approved by the committee, and we'll be sending you a contract."

I said nothing.

"Aren't you excited?" she asked.

"I can't believe this is happening," was all I could say.

How do I explain almost ten years filled with rewrites and tears of frustration? How do I explain my fears that this could never happen?

The Israelites in the desert were also overwhelmed by their fears. The Lord had Moses send some men to explore the Promised Land. All except Caleb and Joshua came back frightened. They described the great size of the people in Canaan: "We seemed like grasshoppers in our own eyes, and we looked the same to them" (Numbers 13:33, NIV).

Their cowardly attitude and refusal to fight infuriated God and earned them another forty years of desert travel. I often wonder how many extra years my anxiety and doubts added. Maybe instead of ten years, I could have completed the book in five.

Conquering unknown territory becomes necessary if we are to move beyond our losses to a new life. We need to take the risk, face our fears, and do what terrifies us. If we don't, we may find ourselves wandering around in the desert for another forty years.

Chapter Twenty-Seven

Courage to Try Again

Did you ever feel overwhelmed by a task, maybe something that wouldn't challenge someone else but scared you to death? Perhaps you even gathered all your courage and gave it a try, but something frightening happened, and you decided never to try again.

I had that experience once.

After the bone marrow transplant, walking was crucial to my recovery. The goal was to start slowly and gradually increase the pace or distance in order to improve my strength. Unfortunately, on more than one occasion, I overdid it and ended up exhausted.

I decided I needed an energy gauge, like the gauge on gas tanks. If the needle pointed near empty, I would be careful not to overextend myself. If it indicated I had half a tank, then I could gently push myself further.

Since such a thing doesn't exist, I had a great deal of anxiety over daily walks. *I could overdo it, exhaust my immune system, and possibly suffer a recurrence of cancer.*

I'm not suggesting this was rational or based on medical facts; I'm only sharing my fears. Remember, I had been told my chances of being alive in ten years weren't high. I wanted to take care of myself. I wanted to live to see Kyle grow up. But I also wanted to get stronger so I could do simple chores like the cleaning, laundry, and errands.

One day in early spring I was so anxious I had to push myself out the door. *Georgia, you'll be OK. Nothing bad will happen. If you try to walk a little each day, eventually you'll regain some stamina.*

Gingerly I walked to the end of my driveway and headed down the hill. I felt the gentle breeze on my face and started to relax. After the harsh winter winds, the mild air reminded me that it was healthy to get outside. I began to feel better.

I strolled along the edge of the road, focusing on the exquisite blue sky. Two birds were sitting together on a telephone wire. Another one was chirping from a nearby maple tree. I took a deep breath, grateful to be alive.

Approaching the yard of a distant neighbor, I noticed that she and her two daughters were playing a game. Emily, the mother, tossed a ball to one daughter, who caught it and passed it on to her sister. A dog I had never seen before was sitting at Emily's feet, following the movement of the ball with his head.

I was touched by the scene. *Now there's a family who knows how to enjoy the simple things in life*, I thought.

Emily caught sight of me and waved.

"Looks like you're having fun," I yelled.

Just then one of the girls tossed the ball to Emily, and she missed it. The ball rolled toward the road in my direction.

Suddenly, the dog jumped up and ran toward me barking ferociously.

In an instant, he managed to dart behind me and clamp his large jaws on my buttock.

I was stunned. It hurt and I wanted to cry.

Emily dashed over, grabbed the dog by his collar, and apologized profusely. "I'm so sorry. Would you believe we just got him from my sister? She complained that he kept snapping at the neighbor's children."

"Well, now you can tell her he bit one of your neighbors," I said half-joking, rubbing my rear in disbelief.

"Come on in." She waved her arm toward the house. "Let's take a look at that bite."

Emily tied the dog while her daughters and I walked to the back door.

Although it was quite embarrassing, we examined the area once we were inside. The dog's teeth had torn through my slacks and broken the skin, leaving a perfect imprint of each tooth.

"I feel awful, just awful," she said as she cleaned the wound, "when I think what you've been through this past year and now this." She applied an antibacterial ointment to the bite.

"I'm sure I'll be just fine," I said for my benefit as well as hers. But my legs were beginning to feel like wet noodles.

Trembling, I started for home. Physically, I was fine. Emotionally, I was a mess.

This never would have happened if you would have stayed at home. This will teach you. Why didn't you take the road to the right? Why did you walk in that direction? Why did you walk at all?

The next couple of days I refused to go outside. I felt safer inside the four walls of my house, protected from the menacing world.

How will I ever be able to take my walk again?

Then a strange thing happened. During my morning devotions, something clicked in my mind. *Well, Georgia, if you believe in God, you'd better start acting like he exists.*

I bolted for the door with determination.

I refuse to let a bite in the butt take away my guts.

My walk went extremely well that day.

Who would have expected a dog bite to cure my fear of walking? But it did! Not only did my anxiety over walking evaporate, but the fact I survived the dog bite gave me strength to tackle other problems.

Unfortunately, none of us are immune to pain and problems, even when we feel we've had more than our share. Loss brings pain. But what might shock you is that growth brings pain, too.

Just when you decide to step out with confidence and take a risk, life might find a way to give you a bite in the butt. After your initial discouragement, it's important to try again. Don't give up, even when it hurts.

Chapter Twenty-Eight

Old Business

I spied them as I hurriedly changed my clothes. Aunt Cecelia was treating me to lunch, and I was running late. But, as I peered into the mirror, that was suddenly the least of my problems.

There on the left side of my chest, where my breast had once been, were a few small pimples that I had not seen before. They looked frighteningly similar to the tiny tumors that had signaled a recurrence two years earlier. I couldn't pretend they weren't anything to worry about. Experience had taught me otherwise. I collapsed on my bed, drained of all strength. *God, please help me! Tell me what to do.*

Reaching for the phone on the nightstand, I called my oncologist's office. "Is there *any* way the doctor could see me this morning?" I begged, explaining my discovery.

"I'm sure we can squeeze you in," the nurse said. "Take your time and drive carefully."

She had heard the panic in my voice.

Shaking and weak, I finished getting dressed and headed for the car, not caring how I looked. I was frightened and my heart was broken.

Still sobbing, I backed out of the driveway to go for Aunt Cecelia. This was one time I wished she knew how to drive.

Minutes later Aunt Cecelia stepped into the car. Seeing my distress, she reached into her purse and handed me a fresh tissue. "Georgia," she said, "you need to calm down so you can drive."

Calm down! How can I calm down? Another recurrence could mean curtains for me.

I broke into another round of tears and wailed, "I never got to Germany!"

"What?" my aunt asked, turning toward me with a "and-where-did-that-come-from" look.

I wondered the same thing, but that didn't stop me from continuing.

"Ever since I was fourteen and saw pictures of castles like Neuschwanstein in German class, I have always wanted to go to Germany. Now I'll *never* get there!" I shrieked hysterically.

"Georgia, you don't know that," my aunt said in a soothing voice, handing me another tissue.

"I was supposed to go before my senior year in the summer exchange program, but because they didn't have enough German families, I ended up in Finland."

"I thought you loved that trip."

"I did. But it wasn't Germany," I lamented, backing down the driveway.

Only God knows how I safely made the forty-minute trip to the doctor's office.

"Come on back," the nurse motioned with her hand, escorting me to an examining room.

Finally the doctor walked in.

"Let's take a look." He examined closely, moving his fingers over the area.

I held my breath. What would he say?

"You know ..." He stopped for a few seconds. "I honestly don't think this is anything to be concerned about."

He moved his fingers over the area several more times. "The pimples don't feel hard like the last time. I'm wondering if maybe these aren't bug bites."

"Bug bites?" I said with a look of shock.

But it was July, and I had been sitting in my garden the day before. "You're serious?"

"Yeah, I think that's what they may be. Keep an eye on them for about ten days, and if they disappear, we'll assume that's what they were," he said, recording his observations on the top page of my thick file.

"Well, if these are bug bites, I'm going to Germany!" I declared.

He looked up questioningly.

"I've always wanted to go to Germany but for some reason never made the trip. After college and marriage, we saved money for a house. Then Kyle was born. Later I went to graduate school and then the cancer and here we are. I guess I could never justify spending money on what seemed like a silly dream. Actually I had forgotten all about it until today."

"Doesn't sound silly to me. Sounds like you have some unfinished business to take care of." He handed my chart to his nurse. "Well, hopefully I won't need to see you until your next scheduled checkup."

"Hopefully you won't," I said as he walked out the door. I quickly dressed and almost skipped down the hall to Aunt Cecelia.

Before I said a word, she knew. My smile gave it away.

"He thinks they're bug bites," I said. "I'm starved. Let's go to lunch."

Aunt Cecelia sighed with relief. "Well, that certainly is good news!"

Within a week the pimples disappeared. Within four months, I stood with mouth gaping open gazing at Neuschwanstein Castle. How magnificent!

My dream had come true thanks to an off-season promotion. It didn't matter that it was bitter cold and there were no flowers blooming. I was in Germany!

Many people, like me, have dreams buried deep within their souls. And like me, they have many seemingly logical reasons to keep them there. However, these dreams have a way of suddenly erupting out of nowhere. And you wonder, *Where did that come from?*

Deep within the fibers of your being, you have managed to carry your dream with almost no awareness of its existence. In my case, it was almost thirty years.

When a dream pops into your consciousness, don't discount it even though some of your past dreams may have been shattered. When you ignore what was important to you in the past, part of you will say, "I had dreams before, and they didn't change anything." No matter how silly they seem, dreams need to be recognized.

Take a few moments and recall some of your dreams. What did you always yearn to do? If they're no longer your heart's desire, let them go. But if they're still important, take the risk, and make them happen.

Taking care of old, unfinished business keeps us true to ourselves. It also fuels us forward toward a new life and new dreams, like going to Germany when the flowers *are* blooming.

Chapter Twenty-Nine

New Business

There are many ways God can plant his vision in our hearts and minds. In 1990, he gave me a dream one night that changed my life.

In the dream, I traveled with a group of nuns to a distant place that I had never visited. The exact location wasn't clear, but I knew I didn't want to go there. I wanted to be home with my son. Nevertheless, we arrived at a camp, or retreat, where there were more nuns. I felt so uncomfortable, like I had no business being there.

One of the nuns said to me, "You are to give a speech this week."

I was stunned. *A speech? Why me? I don't have any message. What can I say that these nuns don't already know?*

But she would not take no for an answer.

Terrified and trembling, I gave a presentation. After the talk, many of the nuns came up and told me how I had touched their hearts.

Suddenly I experienced an overwhelming sense of peace and joy and thought, *I'm finally, finally doing what Jesus wants me to do.*

145

Then I awoke.

Isn't that just great! I'm to be a nun! I can't wait to I tell my son!

But that didn't make sense. I'm not Catholic.

Turning on the TV for distraction, I found Dr. Schuller nearing the end of a message on having the courage to follow our dreams.

Now I was really upset! It was bad enough to dream about being a nun, but now I was hearing that I should follow my dream.

The program concluded with an advertisement for the International Women's Conference on Possibility Thinking, the theme of which was "Stretch and It's Yours!" The commercial said, "As women we need to stretch into the nineties and achieve our *dreams* personally, professionally, and spiritually."

I froze at the mention of the word dream and broke out in goose bumps—holy goose bumps.

I knew exactly what I was supposed to do.

God wanted me to go to that conference. Then I began to wonder if the "nuns" in my dream could symbolize spiritual women, women of God? Could Garden Grove, California, be the unknown place? I had never been there.

I copied down the phone number and called for a brochure. When the information arrived a week later I prayed, "God, show me why you want me to go to this."

As my eyes glanced over the pages, a seminar entitled "Stretch and Write a Book" taught by Marilyn Heavilin, who was introduced in chapter four, seemed to jump off the page. *That's it!* I thought. *That's why I'm to go.*

For the last four months I had been working on a book outline. *God, now I understand! You want me to go out there and meet Marilyn Heavilin. She'll introduce me to a publisher; my book will get published and become a best-seller; and maybe I'll become rich and famous.* (These were *my* dreams, not God's!)

Several months later I arrived at the conference and asked Marilyn to review the outline of my book. "Looks good—keep working on it," she said.

"Can you give me any specific comments?" I asked.

"No, you have a good start. I would suggest you keep working on it."

God, you sent me the whole way to California, and I had to take money out of my savings to hear "Looks good—keep working on it." This can't be! Something is wrong.

Turning to Marilyn, I said, "You don't understand. You are to tell me something."

She looked puzzled.

"I know I was supposed to come to this conference and attend your seminar," I said very boldly. "You are supposed to tell me something!"

She sat back, obviously uncomfortable, and after a long pause, said, "Well ... tell me about your relationship with God."

"Oh, I don't know what I would have done without him during these last few years," I replied.

Then I told her about my bone marrow transplant and the vision I had of Jesus carrying my limp fevered body in his powerful arms.

With tears in my eyes I added, "*Never* have I experienced such a love and comfort as I did that day."

"Sounds like Jesus was with you in the tough times," she said. "Tell me about your daily relationship with him."

I said nothing.

Instantly it hit me; I didn't have a daily relationship with

Jesus. I had grown up in a Christian family. Each Sunday we went to church. I cleaned the pastor's house, babysat the pastor's children, was active in youth fellowship, and sang in the junior choir. But Jesus and God were up there somewhere, removed, distant—someone to call on in times of need.

How had I missed the daily relationship? I felt so foolish. *Why hadn't someone pointed this out sooner?*

"When you go back to your room," Marilyn said, "you may want to pray the prayer to invite Jesus into your life."

As I recorded in my journal the prayer she suggested, I knew *this* was the reason God had brought me to California.

An hour later, I sat on the bed in my hotel room and prayed, "Jesus, I invite you into my life to be my Lord and Savior. Please forgive me of my sins and use me for your honor and glory."

Then I realized that my life had not been centered on God and his glory. It had been centered on me. I recognized there were many other dreams in my heart that were mine, not God's.

Fortunately I discovered on October 11, 1990, that only a life centered on Christ and his vision for me would bring purpose and meaning.

I now realize how staggering the consequences would have been had I not followed that dream. It would have been easy to say, "Well, that was just a stupid dream, why should I go to California?"

It continues to amaze me how God engineered it all. For example, Marilyn, who is a Christian author and speaker, helped me get started in speaking. I had no idea where to begin, but she did.

Oswald Chambers wrote, "Watch for the storms of God. The only way God plants His saints is through the whirlwind of His storms.... If you select your own spot to be planted, you will prove yourself to be an unproductive, empty pod. However, if you allow God to plant you, you will 'bear much fruit' (John 15:8, KJV)."[15]

This reminds us that God often uses the heavy winds of adversity to transplant us. That certainly describes my experience. Uprooted by the storms of health, marriage, and job problems, I now have established roots in a totally new area. If ten years ago you had told me that I would be a speaker and author, I would have said, "You're crazy."

Where has God transplanted you? What dreams has God given you? His dreams, not ours, become the seeds of our new lives. Leigh, of North Carolina, had to learn this truth the hard way. "My husband's business had collapsed," Leigh said, "and money was tight. I took charge and decided I needed to get a job, although we had prayerfully decided I would be a stay-at-home mother to our three young children.

"No matter how hard I tried to orchestrate things, I didn't even get one job interview. It became obvious after months of this nonsense that God had other plans for my family. We ended up moving across the country, and my husband now has a job he loves."

As we rebuild our lives, we need to be careful that we don't tell God where we want to be and what we can do for him.

Taking a risk means establishing our roots where God has transplanted us even if we think we have no business being there.

The following poem, written for my fiftieth birthday, is very special to me:

Georgia

You came to California
To find a spiritual lift.
God brought us together
To give you a special gift.
A gift of eternal life
was what He had for you.
Though you hoped to learn
To write a book or two.
God's plan for you
was of a different kind.
You see, before the earth was formed,
God had Georgia on His mind!
Happy Birthday!!

Marilyn Heavilin 8/21/99

Chapter Thirty

 Too Much of a Good Thing

A lmost every spring, as the daffodils start to fade, I plant my zinnia seeds in the cutting garden. As the tiny seedlings begin to poke their heads up through the earth, I usually discover there are more of these tender little plants than there is room for them to grow.

One year I really got carried away when I sowed my seeds. Rather than ending up with single lines of individually spaced plants, each row contained thick clumps of seedlings, appearing more like grass than germinating zinnias.

As the days passed and more and more seedlings continued to appear, I realized I'd better start thinning. If I waited much longer, the roots of the plants would begin to grow together, making it impossible to remove some without damaging the others.

Yanking out the excess, however, turned into a far more difficult chore than I had imagined.

It was easy to discard those with a yellowish color or the ones damaged by insects, but how was I to choose among the remaining healthy ones?

I planted these and now I'm killing them. How can I know

which ones to pull? What if I pull the wrong ones? Am I allowing the strongest ones to remain? Why can't they all live?

At least I knew the answer to that last question. If I allowed all the zinnias to grow, I would have lots of thin straggly plants struggling for sunlight, nutrients, and moisture. So why was I fighting the process?

I considered this while I worked my way up one row and down another and finally concluded that getting rid of a good thing is hard, especially when it is something I had desired.

As I pulled out the tiny seedlings, I recognized that they weren't the only things in my life that needed to be thinned. My calendar, like these plants, had become crammed with too many scheduled activities. If I didn't do some eliminating soon, each activity wouldn't get the necessary time and attention it deserved.

But canceling appointments and projects proved to be even more troublesome than removing seedlings. Even though these choices were not the life-and-death matters I had confronted with breast cancer, these new decisions sometimes seemed more confusing.

Although I was certain more was not better, my list of good things grew at a breathless pace. There was the writing of my book, the chance to be a producer and interviewer for a local TV program, and more and more opportunities to speak. I had the garden to maintain and of course all the chores and tasks of a single mom.

Please, God, please show me what to do! What needs to go? What needs to grow?

But no sense of direction came. My mind was so cluttered and confused by my hectic schedule that I couldn't hear God's voice. My activities were robbing me of vital energy, and I became resentful, angry, frustrated, and overwhelmed. An innocent question like "Mom, what's for dinner?" could bring a litany of how my best efforts didn't seem good enough.

Early one morning, I pleaded, "Lord, I'm going to become a straggly weak plant that never blooms if we don't do something soon. Help me! Show me what needs to go."

Later the same morning I arrived at the studio to tape a program for *Faith Is Alive*. As my guest and I were waiting for another group to finish, I shared my predicament with him. "I've been praying, but I don't have any peace about it. I want to say no to a leadership position I've been asked to take at church, but it's such an important thing."

"I can't tell you what to do," he said, "but let me share the questions I ask myself when I face that type of situation. 'What's God's plan for me?' and, 'Where will I make the most difference for him?'"

He paused thoughtfully and then added, "Your church may be disappointed with me for saying this, but I think you should focus on your speaking and writing; that's where you'll make the most difference."

I exhaled. I felt a deep sense of peace. He was right. I said no to the position at church and finished up that season with *Faith Is Alive*.

Often, as we plant seeds for a new life, we find ourselves confronted with too much of a good thing. Having sowed heavily, we suddenly find we're spread too thin.

After a barren winter of losses, we're reluctant to remove the new growth, even if we realize it is too much. We're just thrilled that *something* has grown rather than died in our lives.

When John's wife left him—we first met John in chapter fourteen—he found that as a single parent he was on a dead run all the time.

"There were some things I couldn't eliminate, like working

two jobs, fixing lunches, doing laundry, and caring for my three children. But it was the unessential activities, the things I could get out of, that became more numerous," John said. "I attended divorce recovery classes and the singles' group at my church, which had lots of potluck dinners. I snowboarded, lifted weights, and played tennis. After a while I began teaching in the singles' ministry at church.

"Eventually I reached the point where I realized that a few close friends were better than lots of social events. I was worn out by my 'fun hunt.' I got used to being single and settled into a new identity and a new life-style.

"Now I only teach children's church and do short-term missions work. Rather than filling my days with social events, I'm more seriously considering God's call on my life."

Just as the soil can only support a limited number of healthy plants, most of us can only support so many endeavors. Choices must be made. Only the well-tended plants have the best chance of yielding an abundant crop.

When we find ourselves spread too thin, we need to be alone with God and make some decisions. What needs to go? What needs to grow?

Chapter Thirty-One

A Faith Journey

I admit it. I've read the endings of mysteries and novels before I've finished the book. I've sneaked a peek at more than one wrapped Christmas present before Christmas Day. If I date someone more than a few times, I yearn to know how our relationship will develop. Will we eventually marry? Will he break up with me? Will I break up with him? Or will we mutually agree to go our separate ways?

Recently, on a trip home from Florida, I was reminded of the struggle I have with surprises. As I attempted to check my baggage for the return flight home, the ticketing agent said, "I'm sorry, but we've just been informed your connection from Charlotte to Harrisburg has been canceled due to a mechanical problem."

"Oh?" I could feel my stomach tightening.

"I was able to put two people with your itinerary on another flight with a different airline. You would travel through Cleveland. Would you like me to do the same for you?"

"Sure," I said, realizing I would have to resign myself to this unexpected change.

But as I lugged my three heavy bags halfway across the terminal to another airline, irritation replaced my previously serene mood. I didn't like the inconvenience.

After receiving new tickets and calling home to notify my family about the change of schedule, I settled in a quiet area to regroup. *Georgia, it is not the end of the world; unforeseeable things happen all the time.*

As I boarded the flight in Florida, I discovered I was assigned a seat next to a young man. "Hello," I smiled, sitting down and adjusting my seat belt.

"Hi," he replied. "You know, if this flight wasn't full I'd suggest you move to another seat." He stopped to cough, a deep, nasty sounding bark. "I think I have the flu. I feel feverish."

Great! Canceled flight and now I get to sit next to a germ factory.

"Certainly isn't any fun being sick," I said. "I've spent enough days in bed—really don't care for any more."

I silently prayed for us both. *Lord, help him fight the flu, and help me fight my attitude.*

"What was wrong with you?" he asked.

I'm not sure if I was trying to make him feel better or distract myself from my misery, but I proceeded to share the years during and after my bone marrow transplant.

He listened between coughing spells. When I finished he shook his head. "Looking at you I'd never imagine you dealt with all that. How did you manage?"

"Funny, I still wonder that myself sometimes. My faith got me through." Feeling the need to explain I added, "I'm a Christian."

We continued our conversation, and just as the plane landed he said, "Sounds to me like you have too much faith."

Too much faith? How could I have too much faith? "I don't think so. In fact," I responded, "I've often wished I had more."

I could tell he didn't agree. We didn't have time to continue our discussion, so I left with one final comment.

"If someday you face a situation like I did with my bone marrow transplant and loss of job and marriage, maybe you'll think about what got me through—my Christian faith."

"Well, it was certainly nice meeting you," he said, cutting me off in a polite way.

I dashed off to my next connection, since I only had a few minutes between flights. Thirty minutes later, however, I was still waiting to board.

Then the announcement, "The flight from Cleveland to Harrisburg has been canceled due to mechanical problems."

Oh, no! How could this be—two different airlines and two canceled flights in one day?

It was 9:45 P.M. There were no other flights going to Harrisburg that night. I was directed toward a mile-long line at the ticketing counter and labeled a "distressed traveler."

God, I know you're in charge. I know I'm safe and this is no big deal, but I don't like it.

Waiting to make arrangements for another flight and overnight lodging, I overheard the guy behind me say to his wife, "Boy, it just keeps getting worse, doesn't it?" I could identify. I was tired, hungry, and wanted to go home and sleep on my own pillow.

Hours later, as I crawled into bed, I cried, "God, why did this happen? I got up this morning with no thoughts or plans to go to Cleveland. Now I'm spending the night here."

Then I thought about the sick young man on the plane. Was I sent on a missionary journey? But if that was true, why couldn't I have gone right home after my trip to Cleveland?

Sometimes in our travels through life, God rearranges our plans. And he does it without notifying us of the change or the reasons. We end up feeling like I did on the trip home from Florida, as a distressed traveler. We want to feel secure in knowing that things will flow according to our prearranged plans. And we would like to know with certainty how things will turn out.

Unfortunately, one companion on the road to restoring our lives is uncertainty.

Those who have lost a spouse or endured a divorce may wonder, "Will I be able to find someone and get married again?"

The sick would like to know, "Will my health return?"

"Will I get another job that I like?" is a question of the unemployed.

"Will my son or daughter *ever* get off drugs?" some parents ask.

The answer to all these questions is written in calligraphy, framed, and hanging over my desk:

> "God's way is always a faith journey!"
> "In all your ways acknowledge him and
> he shall direct your paths." Proverbs 3:6

Notice it says he will direct us, not give us a detailed itinerary.

"But what if I work as hard as I can and still don't get my teaching tenure?" asked Kathy from Delaware.

Kathy had returned to college in her thirties to get her teaching degree but found herself in a heated battle with the principal during her first year of teaching. The principal threatened not to give Kathy tenure because of her classroom performance.

"It's impossible to please her," Kathy sighed. "I carefully follow the suggestions she writes on my evaluations only to be told a week later I should do it another way. And every night I spend hours on detailed lesson plans that outline every move I make in the classroom. If I knew I wasn't going to get tenure, I'd quit now."

Kathy didn't know, and so she gave it her best; but her best wasn't good enough. Demoralized, Kathy took a year to regroup. The following spring she began submitting applications again.

"Sometimes I think this is all a waste of time," she told me. "I'm spending hours on these forms. I don't even know if I'll *ever* get another job."

Kathy is right. There is no guarantee that she will secure another job, even though she did obtain a long-term substitute position. The only thing she knows for sure is that she has to at least give it a try.

Risk taking often leads to surprises rather than predictable outcomes. We take leaps in the dark with only God knowing where we'll land and the reason why.

But I admit that every now and then I still question God, "So how did I get here?" as I did on my trip to Cleveland.

And guess what? I still don't know his answer to that question.

Chapter Thirty-Two

Out on a Limb

"Enter at Your Own Risk" read the sign posted at the entrance to a wooden walkway. I stood alone and peered into the early morning mist. The walkway led several hundred feet into a swampy area. It looked tranquil and beautiful.

The friends I was visiting were safely occupied back at the house. *Do I really want to go in there?* I hesitated, then prayed, and took a closer look.

The pressure-treated lumber seemed fairly new, solidly nailed with no missing boards. The only obvious hazard I perceived was a lack of side railings. *It would be easy to tumble into the swamp.*

I proceeded cautiously, staying in the center of the walkway. When I reached the end, I stood veiled in a heavy mist surrounded by soothing, still, shallow waters.

Then I spied them—two white cranes quietly feeding along the edge of a thick grove of trees. Mesmerized by their elegant beauty, I lingered and forgot about my earlier concerns of danger. More than an hour later, I safely exited the area.

The sign at the beginning of that walkway could appear in many places. For example, it could have been posted at the entrance to the Promised Land.

Although the Israelites had the promise that God would be with them, they *still* had to face danger. They had to take risks. Before they could settle in the fertile country, they had to fight the Canaanites who already lived there. (See the Book of Joshua.) Some of the Israelites thought the risks were too great.

In the same way, we'll never see the reality of "our Promised Land" unless we are willing to put ourselves at risk. Sometimes we climb out by choice, and other times God puts us out there. Either way it's a faith-stretching experience when we are totally dependent on God.

But there is one major problem when we're attempting to restore our lives. Because we've endured difficult times in the past, we no longer possess the invincible mind-set of a teenager. Instead, we carry vivid memories of helplessness and inadequacy. We have tried hard to change our situation, but we have learned that sometimes our best efforts make little or no difference.

How then, as we attempt to restore our lives, can we plunge into the unpredictable, trusting that all will work out? We can't ignore the hopelessness we felt during our difficulties. Our pain is still too real. We know what it's like to be weak, fragile, and vulnerable.

Why should we believe that life will suddenly get better just because we muster up the courage to put ourselves out there?

How I struggled over these issues! Then one quiet morning, I heard God say, "Georgia, how can I show you my power if you always play it safe? It's only when you go out on a limb that you'll feel my arm supporting you."

But out-on-a-limb experiences can be terrifying! At least that's how I felt during the second event sponsored by Mourning Glory Ministries. I was sure the limb I was out on would break. The plan was to have Tony Campolo speak at our church.

The event was scheduled for November, and we began publicizing it in May. We printed five hundred tickets, decided they would be free, and we would take an offering to cover expenses.

Within two weeks all the tickets were gone.

Trish, who fielded calls for the affair, phoned me, saying, "Georgia, we have a problem. People continue to call, begging for more tickets. I feel so bad. I started a waiting list, but it's huge already. This is only May. What are we going to do?"

We brainstormed. Trish decided to check into the availability of a larger facility.

She called a few days later, "I've found a place! It seats twelve hundred. Get this. They only had one date left this year. And it just happens to be the same date as our event!"

"You're kidding! Where is it?" I asked.

"The Strand Theater."

"Oh," I said, thinking about the exquisite historical theater in our city. "And how much does *that* cost?"

"A lot!"

Now we had an even bigger problem. It would take all of the money in our treasury just to cover the down payment required for the theater rental. Could we count on an offering to pay the remainder of the rental, plus Tony's costs? And how could we charge for the additional seven hundred tickets when the first five hundred were free?

We told the rest of our committee and asked them to pray about it.

The next day on my way to a doctor's appointment I passed a field of grazing sheep. Just then I heard the Lord saying, "Feed my sheep."

"But, Lord, we don't have the money to cover all the costs."

Again he said, "Feed my sheep."

I moaned. I knew what we would have to do—climb out on a limb.

At our next committee meeting we agreed to rent the theater and give away the other seven hundred tickets. We would trust God to provide through the offering.

But unlike Joshua, who with quiet confidence led the armies into the Promised Land, I spent many sleepless nights. *What are we going to do if we don't get the money from the offering? I don't have enough to cover our expenses.* I tossed and turned and worried.

For weeks before the event I'd burst into tears over insignificant things. Then the day before the event, as I continued to fret, my car hit a patch of ice and crashed into a fence post breaking one of the door windows. I was safe but really shaken.

"Georgia, you need to trust God," committee members reminded me. "He'll provide."

"But what are we going to do if we don't get enough money?" I asked.

"We will. We don't need a Plan B," they said.

But I wanted a Plan B! *What if this limb breaks?* I wanted a safety net!

Of course, no net was needed. We not only met all our expenses but also had enough money to rent the theater for the following year. The evening touched many hearts, and for weeks we received thank you notes for our efforts.

Looking back, I'm embarrassed by my lack of trust, but I also know that many other people share these feelings of doubt and insecurity. One said, "I know deep down I want to do this [take the risk and build a new life]. But I also know because of what life has taught me that I can't. I'm just going to have to step out and trust God. But I know I can't do it alone."

God doesn't expect us to take that walk without him. In spite of what has happened in the past, we need to be adventurous and daring—to "enter at [our] own risk." Whether we find two lovely white cranes or receive a bountiful offering, most often we will find more than we expect.

So take a chance—climb out on a limb—and when it doesn't break off, remember whose arm held you up.

Chapter Thirty-Three

Mistakes Will Happen

I stared at the limp brown-tipped clematis vine I had just planted, wondering if it would survive.

I had tucked in worse-looking specimens that had somehow managed to flourish.

It just needs a little extra coddling, I concluded.

Throughout the summer and fall, I made sure the roots were shaded by nearby plants and that the vine was growing in full view of the sun. (This is what makes clematis happiest.) I tended to its desire for a constant level of moisture by making sure the ground didn't get too dry.

When I was rewarded with only a hint of new growth, I declared, "Next year you're on your own."

Early the following spring I decided to concentrate on weeding. The previous season a few of the unwanted plants had managed to grow to the size of shrubs before I had a chance to remove them. I didn't want to repeat that experience.

With my bucket and digger I became a weed machine on a mission. Dandelion, clover, and chickweed were the most obvious, but anything I didn't recognize came out.

That is, until I found myself holding a fist-sized root ball with a few green sprouts. "Ohhh," I realized too late, "my clematis!"

Quickly I attempted to rebury it, hoping the disruption

wouldn't be noticed. But that was the end of that clematis. It never came back.

Sometime later I shared this incident with a friend who replied, "I did the same thing with my clematis a couple of years ago—thought it was a weed."

She made me feel much better.

But to be honest, that's not the only plant I've destroyed through the years. I've managed to do the same to a small butterfly bush and one of my delphiniums. Each time I've given myself a verbal whipping.

"Why can't you be more careful? Don't be in such a hurry! Keep your mind on what you're doing."

When people visit my garden each year, I hear oohs and ahs along with comments like, "What a paradise! This is gorgeous! You must have a green thumb."

These people only see the lovely flowers. Unlike me, they aren't aware of what went wrong.

Mistakes are part of the growing process, whether they happen in a springtime garden or in the springtime of new beginnings. Rather than becoming paralyzed and distressed over failures, we need to learn from our misdeeds.

In life, some of our mistakes are trivial, like my error with the clematis. But some have more serious consequences.

Ray, whom I met at a conference, told me he remarried after grieving over the loss of his wife of twenty-five years. "Four months after our wedding," Ray said, "I made the mistake of not sharing my true feelings about a health problem."

Ray's face was permanently scarred from thirty facial surgeries for skin cancer. But, since it wasn't life-threatening, he hadn't taken it too seriously. However, shortly after the wedding, his doctors informed him that the cancer had crossed over into his lymph nodes.

"I was scared to death," Ray said, "but I didn't tell my wife the seriousness of my condition or how scared I was. She, however, sensed something was wrong and began having stress-induced health problems. Finally, after about five weeks, I realized our 'we-centered' marriage had become an 'I-centered' one because I hadn't been honest."

Ray shared his fears as well as his prognosis with his wife, and their relationship was restored. He has learned that "when you do not trust and do not totally share with your loved ones, you're getting into trouble." Today, six years later, the two of them lead "Engaged Encounter Weekends," encouraging other couples who are preparing for marriage.

No matter how grieved we become over our foul-ups, we need to remind ourselves that mistakes will happen. Watch a child attempt something for the first time, and you'll recall that bloopers are part of growing up. Improvement usually comes with repeated attempts and much practice.

When I first began speaking to groups, I anguished over my errors, such as mispronounced words. My excessive desire for perfection sent me to the pit of despair, and I was sure I should quit.

Then one day Kyle read the Bible aloud to me for the first time. It was Psalm 91 and he mispronounced "buckler." He stopped, anxiously looked at me, and asked, "Does God mind? Is he upset?"

Is God upset that you mispronounced a word? That's probably the furthest thought from his mind!

"Kyle," I said, "he is thrilled that you are reading from his Word. I bet the angels are clapping right now."

No sooner had those words come out of my mouth than I realized I hadn't been nearly as gentle with myself over my first speaking attempts.

Too often we do not risk trying something for fear we will make a mistake and look stupid. Like working in my garden, restoring our lives does not depend on a flawless performance. Rather it rests on God's ability to make something lovely out of all our offenses.

Frustrating, blunder-filled beginnings can result in sweet, sweet endings. Today you will find a flourishing clematis vine climbing up the post of my mailbox. For years I didn't plant another one because of my mistake. Then last year I found a clematis on sale at a garden shop. I took the risk and tried again. Now every time I get my mail, I'm reminded that when I slip up, I don't have to give up.

Reflection From the Garden

We need to remember that gardens forgive. As long as another flower is planted where the dead one was, no one will notice there was ever a problem.

However, before dashing out to buy another annual or perennial, we should determine what went wrong.

- Was the new plant in a weakened state?
- Did it get too much water?
- Was it too dry?
- Was it shaded by another plant?
- Does the soil need fertilizer?
- Did we plant when it was too hot or dry?

Sometimes we just need to try the same thing again. Last year we only received about one-half inch of rain the first month my zinnia and cosmos seeds were in the ground. I tried to keep them moist, but the scorching sun made that difficult. The straggly looking rows that finally appeared only had one or two wilted plants every few feet.

Late in June, I reseeded the entire cutting garden, a first for me. Fortunately, there were several soaking rains soon afterward.

Two months after the second planting, I gave my mother an exquisite bouquet.

"Your zinnias were never so large and lovely as this year," she commented.

I smiled. "They *are* spectacular! But I had to plant them twice."

Part Five

Share Your Gifts With Others

A generous man will prosper;

he who refreshes others

will himself be refreshed.

PROVERBS 11:25, NIV

Chapter Thirty-Four

Morning Glory Seeds

Morning glories!" my friend gasped. "I haven't seen them for years. My grandmother used to have them climbing up her front porch. I remember how the vines filled with flowers in the morning and then the blooms would shrivel in the hot summer sun." Catching her breath, she turned toward me and asked, "Would you share some of your seeds with me?"

"Sure!" I answered. "I'm going to collect some for myself. This is my first year for morning glories. They've become special to me."

In the fall when the vines became brittle and the papery capsules split open, I gathered the small, hard, dark brown seeds. Some fell on the cement steps, others were scattered on the ground, and thousands still hung from the withering vines. I collected enough to share with everyone who wanted some and still had five bulging envelopes left for myself.

I wouldn't have needed to collect my own, for when the ground warmed up the following spring, hundreds of the fallen seeds germinated. Morning glories sprouted in the cracks of the cement walk. Morning glories popped up under my rose bushes and around the boxwoods. Morning glories peeked through dying daffodil stalks. Morning glories were everywhere!

After pulling out all but a few of the seedlings, I faced another morning glory dilemma. What should I do with the hundreds of seeds I had so carefully collected?

I chuckled. Only one year earlier I had wondered how to use *one* packet of fifteen seeds. How quickly they had multiplied!

I knew I couldn't throw my new seeds away. They weren't just any seeds. They were the seeds from the morning glories that God had used to show me how he can turn the undesirable into something beautiful.

I transferred the seeds into small reclosable plastic bags and stored them in a cool dark place until I determined their fate.

Just as I did not expect my morning glory seeds to multiply so rapidly, I never imagined the abundance of gifts that would result from my troubles. Experience, wisdom, and compassion were just a few of the benefits that I could pass on to others.

But these gifts were not the result of my conscious efforts. Rather they were produced as naturally as the fruit of the morning glory plant.

Often, however, I was not aware I had them or was giving them to others.

Al, the manager of the service center where I take my car, has known me for at least fifteen years, before, during, and after my bone marrow transplant.

"There's something I've been wanting to tell you," Al said one day. "I'm retiring in three months and ..."

"Ohhhh," I moaned. Al had always taken good care of my car.

"I wanted you to know," he continued, "that many times when you brought your car in, I would be upset with all the hassles at work. I'd take one look at you, think what you were facing, and say, 'Al, you don't have any problems at all.'" He lowered his voice and added, "You'll never know what a gift your bright spirit was to me. Thank you."

I stood there stunned as I held back tears. He was right. I never had a clue. In fact, the first few years I knew Al I thought he didn't like me because he seldom talked. Later I understood how deeply he cared. He was just a man of few words.

Even if we are aware of reaching out and sharing our gifts with others, our actions are usually a gradual natural result of our circumstances. It is a process similar to a seed evolving into a seedling which develops its root system and later produces blossoms. Just ask Carmen, whom I met while speaking in Alabama.

Several years after her husband's diagnosis of Huntington's disease, Carmen wrote a few essays about being married to someone with this terminal neurological disorder. After posting them on a friend's web site she was flooded with e-mail messages. People asked permission to give the stories to family, friends, and doctors and to use them in newsletters, for school projects, and at funerals.

"From the response, I realized there was a need for a book of personal stories," Carmen said. "I felt like Kevin Costner in *Field of Dreams.* Instead of 'Build it and they will come,' I thought, 'Write it and it will be published.'"

With only a handful of essays, Carmen's son helped her create a web page announcing the release of *Faces of Huntington's* in exactly one year. "I had no idea how this would happen," Carmen explained, "but after much prayer I felt God telling me not only to write the book but also to self-publish. Since our medical bills had depleted our savings and put us in debt, this seemed impossible."

Then one day Jim (not his real name) called to order twenty-five copies of the book for Christmas. Jim's wife had Huntington's disease and was one of those featured in the developing book. Carmen informed him that the book wouldn't be ready until spring, and first she had to presell enough copies to pay for publication.

Sadly, within a few months, Jim's wife died. He and Carmen continued to communicate over the Internet. Later he surprised her by calling and saying, "I want to pay for the first printing of *Faces of Huntington's.*"

"Thank you so much for your generous offer," Carmen said, "but I don't think you can afford it."

"My wife was so honored to be featured in the book," Jim said, "that I want to make sure it happens. This disease has received so little publicity over the years, and you have spent a year writing and rewriting, so this is the least I can do. The money from my wife's insurance policy will cover it."

Eventually Jim and Carmen decided on a no-interest loan for the book, and he sent a deposit to the publishing house. Nine months after the book's release, Jim was paid in full.

Carmen didn't set out to write a book nor did Jim plan on spending thousands to have one published. Their unwanted gifts naturally contained "seeds" for them to share.

Remember those stored morning glory seeds? I decided to share them with my audiences when I spoke. I told the story of my unwanted gift from Aunt Cecelia, and then I passed on the next generation of seeds. Here's a letter I later received:

Dear Georgia,
You do not know me, but I attended the women's conference where you spoke. At your presentation you gave out

seeds for morning glories. At the time, I thought how nice but I won't plant them because I do not have a green thumb.

Well, in early summer I thought why not. Here goes nothing. Much to my surprise blossoms are beginning to bloom each morning. It is a wonderful sight, and even though I don't know you I think of you daily whenever I look out my window and see the rich green vines and purple blooms.

Thank you for sharing a small part of yourself. I hope your health continues to be good.

In the meantime keep spreading your seeds of kindness. I'm really enjoying their beauty.

Chapter Thirty-Five

Small Treasures

W ould you like this turkey wing?" a petite white-haired woman asked, holding out a seashell.

Surprised, I looked around to see to whom she was talking. My friend who had come with me to the beach was nowhere in sight. Several serious shell collectors bolted past the two of us. More than one person had darted ahead of me that morning attempting to be the first to search an area.

Yet this elderly lady, wearing a bright red jacket, was offering me a wonderful shell.

"Why thank you," I said, amazed by her generosity. I examined it closely. "It's perfect."

"Yes, the shape and its brown and white markings certainly remind you of a wing on a turkey, don't they?" Then she added as she walked away, "It's the largest one I found today!"

I stood there, deeply touched. Here in the midst of the race for the perfect find was a lady who chose to give away one of her treasures.

Later, as I was washing the sand off my shells, my friend returned from her excursion. "You're not going to believe this," she said with excitement. "But I was walking along the beach, and this lady came up and offered me a perfect conch shell."

"Was she wearing a red jacket and carrying a cloth bag?" I asked.

"Yeah, how did you know?"

"Because she gave me a large turkey wing!" I laughed.

"Wow! I'm impressed," my friend said. "What a neat lady!"

Although we never saw her again during our brief stay at the beach, we were both affected by her kindness. The gesture of sharing one shell and a bit of knowledge was in direct contrast to the competitive spirit of the rest of us who greedily gathered our piles.

The next morning my friend and I decided to imitate her by sharing one of our special finds with someone on the beach.

In a world filled with needy and greedy people, it is easy to become overwhelmed and say, "Why even bother? My attempts to help others are hopelessly inadequate." Yet, like the lady on the beach, I sometimes discover that I've made a difference when I do what I can.

Recently, after a phone call to my friend Rosene (introduced earlier) who was dealing with her teenage daughter's poor choices, I received this card:

Georgia, it was so good to get your phone call this past weekend and to know that someone actually knows me, understands me, and still loves me!

I love your e-mails, too. You understand how much just one small kind gesture can mean to someone sinking in the mire of despair. I just want to let you know how very much I appreciate your thoughts, your prayers, and your friendship!

Rosene

Unfortunately I *had forgotten* "how much just one small kind gesture can mean." Her note was a good reminder.

It only took one encouraging conversation to lift Joyce's spirits after a difficult move. With her husband's retirement, they had sold their home of forty years to move closer to two of their children.

"After lots of tearful good-byes, we left San Diego," my friend Joyce said. "Before we entered the state of Nevada we sat by the Walker River and prayed together. We thanked God for the years in San Diego (we came as newlyweds and left as grand-parents) and then headed to Reno, the place we now call 'home.'"

About a week later Joyce and her husband met a couple in a restaurant. "We got to talking, and would you believe they left San Diego only two years ago?" Joyce told me excitedly. "They talked about all the positives they've seen in their move to Reno. They love it here!"

Sandy, whom I met at a conference in New Orleans, is a great example of someone who doesn't let impairments hinder her from doing what she can. When Sandy was seventeen, half of her tongue was removed because of cancer. Although speaking is difficult, Sandy, now in her forties, teaches Bible study classes. One of the women at her church said, "Sandy loves the Bible and teaches it with boldness and passion. She has moved many hearts including mine."

There is no service or gift too small. Whether it be one shell, one call, one conversation, or one Bible study, we can make a positive difference in the lives of others. And when we show we care, maybe, just maybe, someone else will be inspired to do the same.

One Loving Act

If I can stop one heart from breaking,
I shall not live in vain;
If I can ease one life the aching,
Or cool one pain,
Or help one fainting robin
Unto his nest again,
I shall not live in vain.

Emily Dickinson

Chapter Thirty-Six

Sharing the Burdens

I hurried to answer the phone.

"This is Cathy," a trembling, terrified voice said. "I have cancer." Then I heard nothing but heart-wrenching sobs. "Am I going to die?"

"Oh, Cathy, I hope not. What kind of cancer?"

She didn't answer, just continued to cry. Finally I detected something about the uterus and picked up the words "I need a hysterectomy" in the midst of more wails of distress.

"I'm afraid I can't handle this," Cathy said. "Am I dying?" she asked again. "Is it all through my body?"

Not waiting for my answer she continued, "I just called my parents. I don't know why I called you next."

Admittedly Cathy and I weren't best friends, but I knew why she had called me. Who better to share her misery with than someone who had endured the same verdict? The depth of our friendship wasn't what was most important. At that moment she needed comfort and knew I could sympathize with her deep pain. How my heart ached for her.

In the days ahead I called her frequently. There was the usual battery of blood tests, X-rays, and decisions. "I just want my normal life back," Cathy said.

That one statement flooded me with memories. I thought of times when I wondered if I would ever have a life that didn't involve doctors, nurses, technicians, medical centers, or hospitals. I remembered never being able to plan ahead for fear I'd be too sick or too weak.

After Cathy's surgery, I visited her in the hospital. Her spirits were good, as she lay surrounded by beautiful floral arrangements and lively company. But I struggled with feelings of helplessness brought on by the sights, sounds, and smells of the hospital.

I continued to keep in touch with Cathy, especially after her doctor visits began to taper off. There were times I wanted to fix her problems, times I wondered if I had said the right thing. But in the end I had the strange feeling that by helping Cathy, I had helped the confused, overwhelmed, frightened me of years ago.

In his play *The Angel That Troubled the Waters*, Thornton Wilder wrote, "In Love's service only the wounded soldiers can serve." It is the wounded and brokenhearted who have experienced the sorrow that teaches compassion and the pain that teaches understanding.

A dear friend, Dianne Waggoner, sent me this poem after the death of my stepfather. Would her words have been so consoling to me if I hadn't known she had also lost someone very special?

I cannot remove the pain of death or bring a loved one back to life.

I cannot explain God's plan or even pretend to understand.

I cannot tell you that your loved one has gone to a happier place, without knowing it now makes earth the saddest place.

But, my dear friend, I can tell you that there is a time you will heal and the devastating pain won't always be so real. I can weep with you when you weep and stay to dry the tears when you can't sleep.

I can tell you that your loved one fought the fight and kept his faith and now it is your turn to finish the race.

Most people who endure difficult times develop tenderness toward the hurting. How can we be complacent? We experienced God's love and were cared for in the midst of our distress. Now, as Paul reminds us in 2 Corinthians, it is our turn. "The Father of compassion and the God of all comfort" (2 Corinthians 1:3, NIV) has comforted us so that we may comfort those who are suffering.

But isn't mourning with those who mourn painful at times? You bet it is. However, the only other choice we have is to be indifferent to their despair.

Following are a few of the many women I've met who endured devastating losses and later chose to bear the burdens of another.

Jerry, from North Carolina who was introduced in chapter seventeen, lost her only two sons in an accident in which one of them was the drunk driver.

"Sharing with other Christians who are traveling down my road turned out to be one of the most helpful things," Jerry said. "At first I didn't want to tell people that my son was drunk. I was afraid they would think he was a bad person. But now, I speak about making good choices in schools, and I visit, pray with, and listen to other bereaved parents. I allow them to share their pain, and I watch how God works in their lives."

In 1994 Jerry received the "volunteer of the year" award from MADD.

Lisa from Maryland was in her thirties when doctors discovered she had lupus. "I couldn't stand up long enough to do the dishes or play with my baby for any length of time," Lisa said. "But I learned to live at a slower pace and depend on daily medication to feel 'normal.' Eventually I was able to determine what triggered my symptoms and began to take some preventative measures."

Later Lisa, a counselor, started a "chronic illness" support group to help others. She empathizes with her clients' ailments because she knows firsthand "the fatigue that 'goes through the bone' like the wet wind of a gray winter day."

At the age of thirty-six, Carol, who was introduced in chapter sixteen, said of her transplant several years earlier for breast cancer, "I think the most important step I took was to shift my focus from myself to what I could do for others. I visit breast cancer patients through Reach to Recovery with the American Cancer Society and speak at women's groups like MOPS [Mothers of Preschoolers]."

When Marjorie, from New Jersey, was thirty-four, her marriage suddenly ended, leaving her to raise her three-month-old daughter alone.

"Knowing Jesus was there in the middle of the night when the tears flowed, kept me from going over the cliff of despair," Marjorie said. "I learned how important it is to listen no matter what time of the day or night. Now I tell folks who are distraught to call me *anytime* to talk."

Laura Beth, whom we met in chapter twenty-two, said about the delivery of her stillborn daughter, "I realized through my experience that I was not the amazing, self-sufficient super woman, serving Christ with gusto, that I'd always worked so hard to be. I was weak, needy, and susceptible to life's blows.

"Whenever I hear of a woman who lost a baby," Laura Beth continued, "I write her a letter based on my experiences and God's wisdom, whether I know her personally or not. Several women have responded that this correspondence was one of their greatest sources of comfort, that someone truly understood."

Leslie, whom we met in chapter nine and whose daughter had been murdered, sent me a letter in which she wrote, "I recently contacted a young lady outside of Austin, whose four-year-old son had been killed by his father who then committed suicide. It has been such a joy to be used by the Lord in comforting her. The circumstances were so similar to my experience ... I just HAD to reach out!"

Like these women, we need to share the suffering of those around us. We will not only lessen another's burden, but we'll find our once heavy hearts a bit lighter.

Chapter Thirty-Seven

From Pit to Garden

Are you glad you came?" my brother asked with a smile that said he already knew the answer.

I searched for just the right words. "Yes" seemed inadequate. After all, this was a dream come true. For five years, ever since I first heard about Butchart Gardens in Victoria, British Columbia, I had wanted to come. Twice it almost happened and twice my plans fizzled. Then, suddenly, I cashed in my frequent flyer miles, and there we were!

"Inspiring" is what I wrote about my visit in the guest book near the exit. Kyle thought it was "magical." Some wrote "sensational," "mystical," "magnificent," and—would you believe—a few wrote "boring."

Boring? Even if you hated flowers and were dragged there by a flower enthusiast, how could it be boring? Just thinking about the determination it took for one woman in the early 1900s to transform an unsightly fifty-foot-deep limestone quarry into a lush garden energized me.

I wonder if those people who described it as boring ever got down on their hands and knees and struggled to create something lovely. Had they ever grappled with the obstacles and frustrations that one endures in the process?

Guess you can tell "boring" upset me.

As I strolled through the Sunken Garden I tried to imagine what it must have looked like eighty years earlier, "littered with chunks of rock and stagnant puddles."[16] The transformation had begun with the hard labor of gathering those rocks together in designated areas. Then "ton after ton of topsoil was brought in by horse and cart from a neighbouring farm.... A particularly deep portion of the quarry was carefully lined and filled with water to create a shimmering lake fed by a waterfall and stream."[17]

"Mrs. Butchart solved the problem of the grim gray quarry walls by dangling over the side in a bos'un's chair and carefully tucking ivy into any discernible pocket or crevice in the rock."[18]

And then at last the flowers and shrubs were planted.

As my sister-in-law said when first setting her eyes on the sight, "It's hard to describe the sensation of standing at the entrance to the Sunken Garden. The size and all that is there is breathtaking."

Kyle's favorite area was the Japanese garden. He loved the spot where a "porthole" was carved in the shrubs and trees enabling visitors to gaze out at the harbor.

Even my five-year-old niece, Morgan, loved it.

"Can we go back to the gardens?" she asked the next morning.

Like the millions of visitors before her, she was enthralled by the beauty of this world-renowned place.

What amazed me is that "Jennie Butchart, by her own admission, knew nothing about gardening."[19]

Mrs. Butchart's accomplishment encourages each of us to

ponder the bleak-looking areas of our lives, our own unsightly pits.

How can we create something lovely, something worthy of being passed down to our children and grandchildren?

Heather, who shared in chapter two that she once thought only the most tragic losses called for sorrow, created a song. She explained the story behind it in the following letter:

I was grieving because my friend Kim had moved from our Illinois town to Florida. Kim had been an encourager and confidant for several years. There was no question in our minds and hearts that it was the right move. I was genuinely happy for her.

It proved challenging, however, to reconcile this rejoicing with feeling like a little girl whose quivering lower lip testifies, "My best friend has moved away."

Not too long afterward a loss of more tragic proportions was soon to jolt the way I was grieving. On Valentine's Day of that year, a nine-year-old boy, who lived in a nearby town, died in an accident at his home. Tammy, a mutual friend of Kim and me, was Aaron's teacher. Tammy needed support as she faced a roomful of grieving children. She wrestled daily with her grief while trying to help Aaron's classmates work through their feelings.

Tammy's loss caused me to struggle even more over my friend's move. Compared to the tremendous pain Aaron's friends and family must be experiencing, the empty space in my life seemed insignificant. I kept wishing I could handle Kim's absence better.

Though I knew my loss wasn't as tragic as that brought on by Aaron's death, I finally gave myself permission to feel my pain. That April for Kim's birthday, I penned a song entitled "I'd Really Like to See Your Face." It was just an expression of missing someone—no real resolution, just verbalizing the feeling of loss.

That same spring, Tammy asked, "Could you come sing and tell stories to my class?"

I arrived with my usual repertoire of humorous folk tales and silly songs. After forty-five minutes of seeing their faces light up with laughter and hearing their giggling, I was tempted to stick to the safe path. "Quit while they are smiling," my experienced performer voice shouted within me. But a compassionate voice whispered from a wiser corner of my heart, "They need to hear this song. They need to know others experience grief."

I took a deep breath, "I know this has been a hard year for you all since Aaron died...." In unison the children pointed to the wall behind me where Tammy had hung a photograph of Aaron. Every face in that fourth-grade classroom became riveted to mine; they seemed so relieved I would acknowledge their pain.

I told them how I missed my friend, Kim, who had moved. I explained that as I finished writing her song, I thought about how much they must miss Aaron. Then I sang the song.

They listened intently—the room seemed to ache. I closed my program with several upbeat stories and songs that nine- and ten-year-olds usually relish. But the song they asked me to sing again was "I'd Really Like to See Your Face."

One student rose from his seat and passed around a box of tissues. Some of the students held hands while the tears flowed.

A few days later I honored their request to send them a copy of the lyrics. Tammy put them in the center of the memorial bulletin board that the class had created in Aaron's memory. Aaron's parents heard about the song and also requested a recording and a copy of the lyrics.

That song is a testimony that all of us miss someone, somewhere, in some way. If I had believed my pain wasn't big enough to feel, I would have missed the opportunity to receive the gift of a song that has put mourning into words for hundreds of people.

I now include "I'd Really Like to See Your Face" often in school and civic programs, and I am amazed how audiences of all ages seem to grow quiet and listen with their whole being.

Heather Harlan Bacus

Whether we change a quarry into a garden or a broken heart into a song, the question we need to ask ourselves is, "How, with God's help, can I transform the unpleasant and ugly things in my life?"

Mrs. Butchart's legacy encourages each of us to look at "our pits" with vision and make them into something of beauty and hope for others.

Chapter Thirty-Eight

Give What You Have to Give

Flowers often graced the teachers' lunch table in the elementary school where I taught physical education. Betty, one of the teachers' aides, brought us the bouquets week after week.

That was more than twenty-five years ago, but I still recall how impressed I was by her generosity. I don't remember if the flowers she gathered were peonies, roses, or dahlias, but when we fussed over them, she would say, "I just bring whatever I have growing in my garden."

I now understand what I'm sure Betty already knew: one of life's greatest joys is to give of what we have.

To find the gifts we can give, each of us, like Betty, need only take inventory of what is growing in our lives.

Beth had a bone marrow transplant for breast cancer three years after I did. Excitedly, she told me about a devotional book she had written for breast cancer survivors.

"Even though my book, *God Still Sends Rainbows*, isn't published yet, it's got a life of its own," Beth said with eyes sparkling. "I print out the manuscript and give it to anyone dealing with breast cancer. People hug my book," she continued, "like I've just given them hope. The letters I get are amazing. One woman said that my experience taught her to trust God. She wrote, 'When things get tough, Mom and I smile and say, "It's a battle out there, but if Beth can do it, we can do it, too!"'"

"God wanted me to have hope through my pain and suffering," Beth added. "What a joy it has been to pass that hope on to others."

Cindy, who lives in Washington, suffered the disappointment of infertility. "It still takes all my strength to hold a new baby. I so wanted to experience motherhood," she said. For her, Mother's Day is the worst day of the year.

Cindy decided to do something for others who felt left out on Mother's Day. "This year I hosted a tea for women like me who never had children," she said. "We wore hats and corsages and had a great time." Then she added with a smile, "I'm going to do it again next year."

Not everyone can write a book or host a tea, but everyone can give a compliment. As a child, Steve, whom I met at a conference in Washington, yearned for his father's approval. "Hugging Dad was like hugging a telephone pole," Steve said. "I once told him, 'I just hope someday you'll be proud of me.'"

When Steve was in his twenties, his father was diagnosed with brain cancer. "One morning, near the end of Dad's life, I sat by his bed while he slept off and on," Steve said. "He motioned me toward him with his hand. Then he hugged me to his chest in a way he never had before. Even though Dad no longer had the ability to say the words I had wanted to hear, he was able to communicate that he was proud of me.

"Ever since that cherished moment I look for ways to affirm

other people. I try to lift others up because it meant so much to me."

While Beth and Cindy had hope and encouragement to give, Steve offered affirming words. I, like Betty, especially enjoy sharing my flowers.

Recently my mother wanted to deliver some flowers to a friend in a nursing home. "Do you have anything blooming in your garden that I could give her?" she asked.

"I think there are a few black-eyed Susans and some baby's breath," I said.

"If you have time to make a bouquet," she said, "I'll take them when I visit her tomorrow."

A few black-eyed Susans that the insects hadn't mutilated and five sprigs of baby's breath were all I could gather. But when I put them all together in a lovely little vase, the results were stunning.

When we give of what we have—whether it be material possessions, talents, or lessons we learned from our struggles—somehow it ends up being more than enough.

But isn't that what Betty modeled and Jesus taught in Luke 9:10-17 when he fed five thousand people with five loaves of bread and two fish?

Chapter Thirty-Nine

From the Perch of Healing

Why can't you accept it and move on?" a middle-aged woman at the next table said to her friend. "You were content with single life before you met him."

I couldn't help but overhear these two women as I sat, waiting for my friend to join me at the restaurant. It appeared that the one woman had been dating someone for almost a year when he abruptly called to say he just wanted to be her friend.

"I can and will accept it," she stated with conviction. "But I need some time to adjust to this sudden change. I enjoyed our time together. I liked going to dinner and the movies with him."

"Well, you can't sit around and mope about it forever," her friend said.

"I'm not," she defended herself. "This only happened five days ago."

"I just think you need to start seeing someone else," her friend replied. "Then you'll forget about 'what's-his-name.' Remember when Tom and I broke up, how I started to date Ned? I just called and invited him over for dinner. We had fun, and I forgot all about Tom."

At that moment my friend arrived for our lunch, and I didn't hear any more of their discussion. However, later that day I thought how the jilted woman's friend failed to understand there is no immediate cure for sadness. The disappointed woman didn't need someone else to date. She needed time to grieve.

It is no coincidence that "Sharing Our Gifts" is the *last* section in this book. Before we can share with others what we have learned through our difficulties, we need to make sure that we did our grieving, searched for God's perspective, discovered the gifts, and took some risks. As my speaker and writer friend Karen O'Connor found, a whole new perspective comes with recovery.

Years ago Karen's husband left her and their three children for another woman. "After years of anger and bitterness over what my ex-husband had 'done' to me," Karen said, "I realized, by the grace of God, that there was a life lesson in this for me.

"I came to understand that I had made my husband my god, and when he left, I was devastated. I didn't know who I was, what I stood for, or what to do next. And my kids were equally a mess. I was too weak to be there for them in the way they needed."

Years later, after walking with Christ, Karen saw how her experience could help other women going through similar situations.

"By then," Karen said, "I was able to share the events and my recovery from the perch of healing, instead of from the pit of despair.

"If we share our story too soon (while still 'in' it), the focus is on us, our process, our problem, our pain, instead of the mercy and grace of God," she continued. "I believe it's important to keep our counsel with the Lord until he gives us the go-ahead.

Then we can be certain that what we share will not only benefit those who listen to us but honor and glorify him as well."

Karen waited five years before she began writing about her experience. She admits that if she had shared her troubling times earlier the emphasis would have been on what her husband had done to her rather than on what she needed to learn.

Gwen, whom I met at a conference in Washington, also discovered she had more valuable insights to give others *after* she had gone through her own "valley of sorrows."

"When Steve, my beloved husband, died of cancer [not the same Steve as in the last chapter], I was left with a void the size of the Grand Canyon," Gwen said. "Shortly after his death, I enrolled in a class at a community college and met Bob, who was not only good-looking and charming but very attentive toward me. I was surprised by how his attention eased the ache in my heart.

"No longer grieving, I looked forward with anticipation to each new day. Within one week my new friend and I were sitting together for lunch, lingering behind as the rest of the students filtered back into the classroom, and having private conversations. One night after a lengthy phone conversation, Bob came to my home.

"As we sat on the sofa, he leaned over and kissed me, stirring all the passions within. Not only was my husband gone but for a moment so was the pain. How tempting it was to follow my desires.

"But God is good at rescuing his people. Bob and I were interrupted by a phone call, which put an end to what could have been a regrettable event.

"The next day reality slapped me in the face," Gwen recalled. "I asked God to forgive me for trying to bury my pain. The

204 / A Gift of Mourning Glories

ache in my broken heart returned full force, and I was back in
the grip of grief where I needed to be.

"I've learned that when we enter into a relationship prema-
turely, it acts as a temporary pain pill and stops the grieving.
Such a shortcut was not only unfair to Bob but it hindered me
from fully mourning the loss of my husband.

"Experts say it takes two to five years to adjust to a new normal. It took me that long to gather all the pieces of my shattered
heart. Finally I'm at a place where I can give my heart away to
someone else. It was well worth the wait."

Not everyone is like Gwen, willing to be patient and endure
the pain that comes with mourning. Many, like the woman in
the restaurant who was counseling her friend, don't realize that
certain actions, like dating too quickly, can hinder rather than
encourage healing.

This is not to imply that we have to be fully recovered before
reaching out to others. Offering a meal, assisting with errands,
tending our neighbor's children, are all ways we can assist those
who are suffering.

However, it probably isn't wise to counsel others before we
have gathered those insights that come only with time and
heart-wrenching struggles.

How can we hope to lift another up to the perch of healing
if we haven't reached that special place ourselves?

Chapter Forty

The Bright Morning Star

Oh, no!" I gasped.

I had just returned home from a week's vacation, only to be greeted by dried remnants of morning glory vines on one of the railings outside my kitchen door.

In a few weeks television cameras were arriving to tape two programs for the show *Faith Is Alive*. My morning glories were to be a key feature of a segment entitled "Unwrapping the Gifts in Adversity." The plan called for me to record the story of my unwanted morning glory seeds while sitting on the cement steps surrounded by the lush green vines.

I collapsed on the steps and cried, "Lord, now what am I going to do? Even if I replant the seeds they won't cover this railing in time for the show."

A mocking voice, definitely not the Lord's, seemed to say, "Well, let's see if you can find the value in this unwanted gift. You're always encouraging others; now here's your chance to practice what you teach."

Frankly, I wasn't sure there was any value in this situation. I was furious that this had happened the summer the garden was being filmed, but at least I still had mature morning glories on the railing to the left side of the steps.

The next day I pushed my wheelbarrow up to the shriveled remains and closely examined them. Every stalk had been chewed off right above the ground.

The rabbits, I bet!

I blamed them because I had seen them in that area on several occasions.

I dumped an armful of the dead plants into the wheelbarrow and stooped down to pick up a second load. Then something green caught my eye. About a dozen morning glory seedlings, two inches high, were hidden underneath the debris!

Suddenly I experienced a wonderful "ah ha!" moment.

The cameras could show a "before and after" shot of the morning glories!

One side of the steps could show what the vines look like at the beginning of the summer, while the other side would display the morning glories once they covered the railing.

I exhaled. My problem was solved.

This was just one more reminder of how unwanted gifts—troubles, difficulties, losses—continue to appear in our lives. Whether they're minor incidents like chewed off morning glories or major ones like the loss of health, relationships, or jobs, we're seldom prepared for the changes that occur.

Each significant loss in our life must be processed. But we can only do this one step at a time. As we've already seen, the steps toward restoring our life after loss include:

Give Yourself Time to Grieve

This is a time of sorrow and anger, a time of intense emotional pain. We mourn over what could have been until we can let go and accept what happened.

When I gave myself permission to grieve over my losses, there appeared to be no relief for my unceasing pain. The anger was frightening, and the sadness threatened to destroy me. Rather than wallow in my misery or distract myself with a continuous schedule of pleasurable activities, the best approach was to alternate times of pain with moments of relief.

It took much longer than I expected, but finally I reached the point where I was ready to begin again.

Investigate and Observe

Our first attempts to find the positive in our unwanted situations may lead to many dead ends. We create excuses why there is nothing of value in our tragedy. But eventually, having accepted that what once was can no longer be, we focus on the present and the possibilities our "empty basket" can hold.

Initially I was convinced my losses were more than I could handle. But like "seeing" how the railing outside my kitchen door could be a vertical structure for climbing morning glories, I had to look for new opportunities and "see" my circumstances from a new perspective—God's.

Find the Value

As we persevere, we will discover the benefits of our unwanted situation and experience a wonderful moment when we say, "Why didn't I think of that before?"

I was surprised to discover not one but many valued treasures in my adversities. Realizing each day is a precious gift, experiencing God's love and peace in the midst of the pain, readjusting my priorities, and discovering my passion were but a few.

Take the Risk

If nothing in our lives is different after a life-changing experience, then we haven't really accepted our unwanted gifts. Like adding plants to an already established garden, we need to blend our new growth with the valuable experiences of the past.

Mistakes and setbacks are to be expected, but in order to begin anew, fears need to be faced and risks taken.

At first, after my bone marrow transplant, a walk in the neighborhood was a challenge for me. Later, it was conquering the unknown territory of writing a book.

Share Your Gifts

The long, heart-wrenching transformation from surviving to new growth brings an abundance of gifts to be passed on to others. Our experiences, insights, and newfound sense of compassion are but a few.

Today, through Mourning Glory Ministries, I draw on my experiences and reach out to encourage others as they restore their lives, passing on the precious gift of hope.

On June 4, 1999, Kyle graduated from high school. As I sat on the aluminum bleachers that night waiting for the ceremony to begin, I reflected over the last ten years. I remembered the day I was told that the breast cancer had returned. "But I want to live to see my son grow up," I sobbed as one of the nurses held me tightly. "I want to see him graduate from high school."

Now the moment of celebration had arrived. No one in that audience was happier to be there than I. "Thank you, Lord," I kept whispering under my breath. "Thank you for the gift of life." My vision blurred with tears of joy, and the procession hadn't even started.

My deep sense of gratitude, however, stemmed from more

than the fact that I was alive. Although my endurance and stamina were still lacking, compared to those years of utter weakness, my health was great. Instead of a life of emptiness and despair, I now had purpose and hope.

God had restored my life!

To celebrate this event, I wrote a letter to Kyle.

"We made it!" in spite of your learning disabilities and the fact that I was given a 2 percent chance to be alive in 1999.

But we didn't just survive. With Christ, we soared. This year we both signed contracts within a month of each other, a book contract for me and a full college swim scholarship for you.

Nine years ago few would have bet a plugged nickel on that happening for either one of us.

Kyle, I would like to think it was our morning prayer time that made the difference. I would like to think it was our belief in a God who can do the impossible. I would like to think it was our strong wills refusing to stay down even when the count got awfully close to ten. But only God knows the real reasons.

I thank the Lord that together you and I have traveled this far—sometimes hand in hand and sometimes head to head....

When things get difficult (and that's a given), remember life is a gift, no matter how it's packaged. Treasure it. Never take it for granted. And when it ends, I look forward to seeing you in heaven and saying, "We made it!"

The next time you see a morning glory, look at it closely. You will find that the veins in the center distinctly form a five-pointed star. Five can help you recall the number of steps between hurt and healing. Remember: G – I – F – T – S!

And like the morning glory, which produces delicate new flowers each morning, we, too, can blossom anew. With the help of our Lord, the bright Morning Star, we can gradually move from despair and helplessness (mourning) to hope and joy (glory).

But then, didn't the psalmist already write that? "Those who sow in tears will reap with songs of joy" (Psalm 126:5, NIV).

ℛeflection From the Garden

Some of the most helpful gardening tips I've ever received have been from friends or fellow gardeners rather than from books or professionals. Here are a few of them.

- If you want to use gladiolas in an arrangement, cut right after the *first* floweret opens and put in water. Over the next few days they will slowly open.
- Roses and plants like snapdragons bloom on new growth rather than the mature part of the stem. When you cut a fresh or faded flower, prune as far down the stalk as you can.
- Mix coffee grounds with the soil at the base of roses to promote water retention.
- Plant perennials in the fall just before they go dormant.
- Cut off the buds of side stems on plants such as the rose. Although you may not like losing these potential blooms, the remaining blossoms will produce much larger and lovelier flowers.
- Plant Heavenly Bamboo, a shrub that grows to about five feet tall. It provides bright red grapelike clusters of berries in the winter. Add these berries to cut holly and evergreens for a stunning winter arrangement.
- Plant geraniums in clay pots or containers, rather than in the ground, for the best appearance.
- Plant pansies in early fall rather than spring. They will not only give you color in the autumn, but may even have a few blooms in the winter. By early spring they will provide a refreshing burst of color before the daffodils and tulips arrive.

Epilogue

Today Georgia is encouraging others through her speaking and writing. About her suffering and difficulties, she states,

> Although I wouldn't have said this in the midst of my troubles, I now know that I gained far more than I lost. When you allow God to guide you through life's painful processes, he gives you gifts such as peace, inner strength, wisdom, and joy—the joy of knowing him more intimately than you ever could have without the suffering. These gifts are eternal and can never be taken away. They turn our mourning into his glory.

> For our ... momentary troubles are achieving for us an eternal glory that far outweighs them all. So we fix our eyes not on what is seen, but on what is unseen. For what is seen is temporary, but what is unseen is eternal.
>
> 2 CORINTHIANS 4:17-18, NIV

Georgia Shaffer is the executive director and founder of Mourning Glory Ministries, a nonprofit organization whose mission is to educate and encourage others through seminars, retreats, books, and audiotapes.

Georgia is a licensed psychologist in the state of Pennsylvania and has taught for sixteen years in the public schools and at the college level. She also served for three years as producer and interviewer for the TV program *Faith is Alive*.

She has four degrees: an M.A. in Clinical Psychology; a B.S.

in health, physical education, and recreation; a B.S. in elementary education; and an A.S. in computer science.

For information about having Georgia speak at your conference, retreat, or church, to see pictures of her garden, or to attend one of her seminars, please contact:

Georgia Shaffer
Mourning Glory Ministries
P.O. Box 3113
York, PA 17402-0113
or visit the website
www.GeorgiaShaffer.com

Georgia continues to be in remission.

Notes

1. Erin Arentz, "The Momentous Day," *Brio Magazine*, May 1999, 29.
2. Eugene Peterson, *Critique*, 7 (1997), 12.
3. Florence and Marita Littauer, *Getting Along with Almost Anybody* (Grand Rapids, Mich.: Revell, 1998),11-22.
4. Marilyn Willett Heavilin, *Roses in December* (Eugene, Ore.: Harvest House, 1987), 102-4.
5. Heavilin, 105.
6. Patsy Clairmont, *Under His Wings: and other places of refuge* (Guideposts Edition, 1994), 117.
7. "Personal Glimpses—Good Call," *Reader's Digest*, February 1998, 96.
8. Theodore Roethke, *In a Dark Time*, 1964, st. I, as quoted in John Bartlett, *Familiar Quotations* (Boston: Little, Brown and Company, 1908), 874.
9. http://www.oneliners-and-proverbs.com/n_n.html.
10. The spray program was from Witherspoon Rose Culture, P.O. Box 52489, Durham, NC 27717. Information available from Internet web site: http://www.netmar.com/~wrc.
11. Adapted from FAMILY CIRCUS, copyright 1994 Bil Keane, Inc., Dist. by Cowles Synd. Inc.
12. Anna Quindlen, "Exhaust the Little Moment," *Family Circle*, July 14, 1998, as quoted in *Reader's Digest*, November 1998, 64.
13. Source:http://www.johnpratt.com/items/email/1998/learned_bombeck.html.
14. Sydney J. Harris, King Features, *Reader's Digest*, August 1997, 75.
15. James Reiman, ed., *My Utmost for His Highest, An Updated Edition in Today's Language, The Golden Book of Oswald Chambers* (Oswald Chambers Publications Association, Ltd., 1992), March 11 entry.
16. *The Butchart Gardens* (Victoria, B.C.: The Butchart Gardens Ltd., 1997), 3.
17. *The Butchart Gardens*, 5-6.
18. *The Butchart Gardens*, 6.
19. *The Butchart Gardens*, 4.